Praise

'I highly recommend this book to anyone who is interested in becoming a better version of themselves.'
— **Margaux Hackett**, Olympian

'Intriguing, informative and appropriately amusing, *Knowing You* is the chance to explore change and why, even in the face of the deepest self-doubt, it is entirely possible.'
— **Shey Pope-Mayell**, Author

'This book will change your life. Embrace it and let it carry you to new beginnings.'
— **Rosemary Steele**, retired Teacher

KNOWING YOU

The difference that makes the difference

DR. AMANDA FOO-RYLAND

a R^ethink Press company

First published in 2022 by
Panoma Press Ltd
www.rethinkpress.com
www.panomapress.com

ISBN: 9781784529772

Cover image from Pexels.com by Aa Dil

To my beautiful wife, without whom
my life would not be as
rich and wonderful.
Thank you for being who you are.

Contents

Introduction

This is not an introduction.

You will know how to read this book the best way for you. Go with your gut, climb into what feels right.

There are some things to consider, some things I will ask you to think about. Make it your own; dig as deep as you wish or skim the surface.

This book is a little like your fridge at home: you will get out of it what you put into it. Gorge yourself.

1

You Are Here At The Right Time

What made you pick up this book? Was it a recommendation, a gift? Maybe the title spoke to you?

Whatever your reason, the timing is perfect. The fact that you have this in your possession means you are curious and perhaps even ready to learn more about why you are the way you are, wondering what you can do to help yourself. I suspect you may have tried before, made some headway, yet there's still more to do.

People think that change is hard; that it takes time and is expensive. Some people think that change can only come in a pill.

That's an illusion.

Since 2005, my team and I have been helping people create unthinkable change in their lives in as little as three sessions and mainly online. We have worked with thousands of clients, guiding them to uncover what is going on under the radar, to observe and investigate, then to delete beliefs that do not serve them and install beliefs that do.

People think it's magic; it's not. It's just neurology.

Generally, the people we help have tried everything else. They have been medicated; they have tried counselling, life coaching, individual therapy, hypnosis, group therapy and pretty much every type of professional help to allow them to live a better life. When they come to see us, we tend to be the last resort.

Here's why.

People don't know that change can come easily from within. Most think that it is what the coach, therapist or counsellor does for them – does to them – that creates the change, so it is flawed. This is why the client may feel a little better after their session, yet give it a week and they are back to square one. As a result, they believe that they must keep going for more therapy, week after week, sometimes for years; that change takes time and it is hard.

Our clients do the changing. All my team and I do is hold the remote control. We send them questions prior to the sessions and ask them what they have tried before to help them. In most cases, there's such a long list, we call them 'professional clients' – they have tried so much, spent so much time and money attempting to fix the seemingly unfixable.

Timing is everything. Whatever your reason, you are here reading this book right now at exactly the right time for you. It is my intention to take you on a journey to ultimate freedom and it will be much simpler than you may have thought.

You will need to really look at yourself. Become your own detective and you will uncover truths about yourself that will make sense, clear things up for you and allow you to create a happiness and freedom that is probably unimaginable right now.

Ready? Let's get going.

Our mindset makes a huge difference

Let's talk a little about mindset. If you think that we – the therapists, coaches or counsellors – do the doing, make the changes happen in you, you will go away disappointed. This is why the first thing you and I need to do is look at the empowerment mindset.

This is where you look at your life and at some level accept responsibility for it. Let me give you an example of what I mean.

Imagine you're a cork. You are bobbing around in the ocean and find yourself washed up on a beach. It's raining and the sea is grey – best avoided, yet this is where you find yourself.

You say, 'That's OK, I have a dream of living in the Maldives and the ocean will take me there one day. It is just a matter of waiting for the right current to come along.'

You wait and you wait. Each tide takes you back and forth from the UK to Ireland. Back and forth you go. You ride the waves, hoping that one day an external current will take you to your dream location.

It never does. You, the little cork, will get old and find yourself wherever the old corks go, all speaking from a script that sounds something like this:

'I always dreamt of living in the Maldives, it just never happened for me. The current never took me. I wasn't one of the lucky ones.'

Many people spend a lifetime waiting for an external factor to change so that their life can be changed. Winning the lottery; getting a better job; starting a new relationship; their spouse to be more... (fill in the gap);

moving house; making more money; being in better health – you get the picture. Yet it never happens.

External elements don't make our lives better. It is how we take control of our lives once we see that we can take charge, change course; that we are the navigator. Then things start to change.

Life happens for you

A student who came on one of the live courses led by my team and me in New Zealand really loved the concept of being in control and learning from what life deals us. He shared with us that he applies empowerment thinking to his life most of the time; he lives and breathes the empowerment mindset framework.

He was introduced to it many years ago when he was only seventeen and read a book called *Think and Grow Rich* by Napoleon Hill. This iconic book changed his life. He applied the principles of the empowerment mindset and took control. His path changed; he grew; he knew what was good for him, what to avoid. Most importantly, he became the captain of his own ship, not a cork being taken by the tide.

When we are expecting things to change for us, people to change around us, life to deal us a better card, then life is happening to us. We are at the mercy of whatever comes our way and we blame whatever that is for our circumstances. This leads to a blame mentality.

I did this when I got kidney cancer. I defaulted to 'Why me? How did this happen to me?' I was the fittest I had ever been. I had just cycled from Land's End to John O'Groats with two friends, Malcolm and Jonny. For a joke, I'd suggested we threw the National Three Peaks in for good measure, so not only had we cycled the length of the UK, but we had also climbed the height of it.

When I returned to New Zealand, I was having a routine health check. My blood pressure was high so I went to see the local GP, a lovely lady called Tracey. When someone saves your life, you tend to remember their name.

She suggested I take blood pressure tables, which I declined. She could have told me to get on my way for refusing to take the prescriptions she had suggested; instead, she recommended we run an ultrasound.

The truth is, if I'd taken the prescription, I would not be here today.

The truth is, if she hadn't been vigilant, I would not be here today.

I was fortunate. The scan showed a tumour the size of a golf ball in my left kidney. Surgery was planned immediately.

I felt like life was happening to me. How could this be? I was so fit, and yet here I was sitting opposite a urologist and he was telling me I had cancer.

I decided that I needed to think differently. Rather than life happening *to* me, I had to believe that life was happening *for* me.

When we think that life is happening for us, it allows us to look for the bigger meaning. It allows us to look for the learnings from the obstacles in our path, the problems we face along the way, and ask ourselves what each one has been sent to teach us. With this new mindset of life happening for me, I started to look at what this cancer could mean.

With my diagnosis of cancer, people who'd been through a similar illness came to help me. They gave me books that they found helpful, told me stories about people who had overcome the disease. Sometimes they shared things with me that were not so helpful. Not intentionally, of course; they just didn't really know what to say.

I decided to look upon cancer as an adventure I hadn't chosen to go on, but as I was on it anyway, I might as well make the most of it. With the mindset of life happening for me, I was able to look at what cancer was going to teach me. What is around the corner? What can I learn?

This mindset served me really well. As somebody who had never been into hospital before, I found it interesting that when I looked at it as an adventure, I became curious about the experience. Rather than being fearful, I looked at the experience through childlike eyes.

When the anaesthetist came to meet me on the morning of the surgery, she told me she was going to give me a little concoction to make me feel calm. I asked her if I could remain awake and see the operating theatre as I'd never seen one before, apart from in the movies. She clearly thought this was a weird suggestion, but went along with it anyway.

This turned out to be quite good fun. I met with the team that would be operating on me, saw the operating theatre, which was super shiny, and how tiny the table was where the operation would take place. That alarmed me somewhat; I remember asking how on earth I was going to stay put on that tiny table. The anaesthetist told me not to worry.

'The team will strap you down. In fact,' she added, 'why don't you jump on there now? It will make it easier for the team.' That's exactly what I did – I was so relaxed and curious about it all, I hopped on to my own operating table before major surgery.

I don't mean to imply that you must live your life from this mindset the whole time. That would be impossible; as humans, we are emotional beings and sometimes strong emotions can affect our mindset. At a time when fate threw an immense curveball my way, though, the mindset of life is happening for me allowed me to be curious every turn, learning all I could from cancer.

There will be times when you want to blame other people for your circumstances, blame the environment, blame the situation itself. That's OK, but know that while you're in a blame mentality and thinking life is happening to you, then you are powerless. You'll stay stuck where you are. The longer you stay there, the more stuck you'll become.

When my team and I work with clients, we recognise how important it is that they appreciate which mindset they are currently operating from. If they're coming from a mindset of life is happening to them and it's everybody else's fault that they are where they are, then sadly, change will not happen for them. Why? Because they are expecting an external force to do the changing for them – someone else to implement it or an alteration to happen in the environment which will then change their situation.

This is an illusion.

We must take control, as hard as it may seem. Curveballs happen. Life can be going well, and then from nowhere with no warning, it falls apart in a heartbeat. Knowing that we have a choice to be either stuck or empowered, we need to choose the latter as this will give us more resilience than we would ever have believed possible.

Taking the learnings from curveballs

If somebody had tapped me on the shoulder the day after I'd had my kidney taken out and told me that in a year's time, my husband Keith would die of the same disease, I would've told them they'd got the wrong person. There was no way that could be true. He was fit and healthy; I was the one who had just had my kidney removed.

Yet a year and a day later, my beautiful Keith, who I had been with for nineteen years, passed away from stomach cancer.

Once again, I found myself slipping back into the 'life is happening to me' mindset, blaming cancer, blaming the medical team, blaming whoever I could blame to try and ease the pain. As a result, I stayed stuck.

Knowing what I had learned from my own illness, I realised that this is a disempowering mindset. While it might have been tempting to curl up in a ball and stay in a safe zone, this would not do me any favours in the long run. Without coming from an empowerment mindset, I was only going to stay stuck and probably drink a lot of Pinot Noir.

If all you take from this first chapter is the ability to ask yourself what you can learn from whatever adverse situation you find yourself in, then I can promise you this will stand you in good stead. For you to grasp this concept fully, I am going to be vulnerable with you. I have had lots of curveballs sent my way over the last seven years and have used them to learn first-hand what a true empowering mindset is.

In my first book, I wrote about mindset tools for neurology. The book was published in 2012 and back then, my experience was limited to working with clients and helping them to make unbelievable change. The curveballs started coming my way in 2013, and then they came thick and fast. Every time, I applied the 'life is happening for me' mindset and it really has allowed me to flourish and grow. I'm in a much better place than I would have been if I had not applied this mindset.

After I'd lost Keith, I decided that I needed to create the life I wanted without him. This seemed almost impossible after nineteen years of being with my soulmate. Then a life-changing moment happened, one I will remember for the rest of my days.

I was running around the lake in Queenstown, New Zealand with my beautiful friend Vicki when she stopped in her tracks. I almost ran straight into her, she stopped so abruptly.

She explained to me that she'd just had an epiphany, had realised that my life was like a huge canvas. On one side of the canvas was rich textured paint that represented from the point I was born up until the time Keith passed away, and the other side was plain white. It was there for me to paint whatever I wanted as the masterpiece of the rest of my life.

Then she added, 'If anyone's got a toolbox to do this, you have, Amanda.'

I got painting, deciding I wanted to have magic in my life. I wanted to have another partner to travel life with, having realised I was not good at travelling solo.

I'd had three long-term relationships in my life. One when I was young – ten years with a hot fireman. One was a five-year marriage to a national basketball player, and then nineteen years with beautiful Keith, so you would naturally think that my next choice of partner would be a man. Instead, I found myself falling in love with a woman called Sarah, surprising everyone, including me.

Even my own beautiful mum said, 'You're not gay, love, you're grieving.'

Once again, I took the approach that life was happening for me and not to me and asked what I could learn from this. What I learned was that I'm not gay, I'm not straight, I'm not bisexual; I'm Amanda and I just happened to fall in love with a soul who's attached to a female body. This mindset allowed me to live my truth and my life on my terms rather than falling into other people's expectations of whatever they felt I needed.

When you lose your life partner, the advice that comes from family and friends is varied. Take your time; be gentle with yourself; don't make any big decisions while you're grieving – that kind of thing. The truth is that the only person who knows what is right for you, is you. No one else. Asking what you can learn from this situation allows you to see with more clarity what you need, taking responsibility and action. This gives you power.

You might be thinking, 'This is all well and good, Amanda, but what happens if you have an accident? Something totally out of your control? Can you really have this empowerment mindset when what's happened is not your fault at all and there is someone else to blame for it?'

In the past, I struggled to answer this question. Not now, though.

Just be you

Sarah is a wonderful human being. She loves personal development, loves life and is a loving person. She is exactly the right person for me, and I for her.

We planned to marry at a vineyard in Portugal. First, though, we went on a fundraising bike-ride challenge, cycling from Courchevel in France to York in the UK: 1,000 miles in ten days in terrible weather. It seemed like a great way to ensure we'd be able to fit into our wedding dresses.

Off we went. On the last day of our challenge, 5 June 2016, we were due to cycle from East Anglia to York, 100 miles to the finish line. We woke up early to lots of missed calls.

Sarah's beautiful sixty-year-old mum, Doreen, had been diving in Perth, Western Australia. It was her usual Sunday morning dive with her friend and dive buddy, John. They had dived that site ninety-six times according to her dive log.

This time, Doreen had been attacked and killed by a great white shark.

You have more chance of being killed by a vending machine.

Sarah was in such shock that it took around four minutes for me to establish what had happened. She was unable to tell me; it was as though she believed if she didn't speak it out loud, it wouldn't be true.

We then went into planning mode. We needed to get to Perth to be with her family as soon as possible.

When I entered the breakfast room in our hotel to tell our support team that we needed to fly to Australia immediately, there it was all over the news: 'Grandmother Killed by a Great White Shark'. It was true; it was devastating; it was cruel; it was unfair. It was a month before we were due to marry.

Losing Doreen was hard. She had been so excited that her only daughter was getting married and she knew we wanted to have children; she could not wait to be a grandma again. Doreen had been a lecturer at Edith Cowan University in Perth, teaching neonatal nurses; babies were her passion. Sarah called her the baby whisperer.

We now have twin baby boys and there is not a day that Sarah does not wish her mum was here to support, celebrate, love and cherish them. We cannot change the cruel facts; what we can change is how we respond to them.

Sarah immediately looked at what this could teach her. How could she grow and learn from this tragedy? How could she use her learnings to help others?

As a result, she raised money for a scholarship set up in Doreen's name for single parents to train to become neonatal nurses at the Edith Cowan. It is a great success; year after year, people who could not otherwise have afforded this have been able to connect with their passion.

Sarah has trained in neurolinguistic programming (NLP), Timeline Therapy™ developed by Dr Tad James in 1984 (this therapy deletes negative emotions and works with phobias and goal setting) and hypnosis. She has the tools to help her move from the grey bubble and take personal responsibility for how she responds to difficult situations. We like to say that responsibility is knowing that you have the power and ability to respond in the way that you choose. This is the true meaning of responsibility.

We got married on 7 July 2016, a month after Doreen had died. Sarah said her mum would kill her if she cancelled the wedding. We had a beautiful day and, as painful as it was, we remembered Doreen, talked about her, laughed and cried.

We went to Burning Man on our honeymoon. This is an amazing one-week event held in the desert near Reno, Nevada, which attracts more than 80,000 people. During this week, Reno becomes the third largest city in Nevada. To Sarah and me, it represents humanity at its best, as the whole foundation of the event is based on gifting, looking after each other and giving without receiving. Once we got back to civilisation, I asked Sarah what she had learned by losing her mum in such a shocking way. She gave it some thought while sipping her dirty martini.

After some time, she said, 'I have learned to just be me. The person who knew me the best is no longer here, so I need to be me, trust me. I know what is best for me, I always have done, but I only realised this now. One more thing: life is short.'

Great learnings from something so horrific.

We acted on these learnings, creating an online course to give others the tools that helped us to go through with our wedding, navigate the trauma and live life the best way we could. We call it 'Just Be Me' and it's free. Around 4,500 people have completed the course and thanked us for creating it – the link is at the back of the book for you.

Life is not about whose fault it is, who we can blame when things don't go our way. Sarah and I don't spend our days hoping the shark dies. If we did this, then we would remain stuck. It's like drinking emotional poison every day. The only life that dies from a blame mentality is ours.

Now it is your time

If you are reading this, then now is your time. You were meant to learn this today. It is a gift that will enhance your life; trust me, I have seen it first-hand.

Ask yourself, 'At some level, this learning has been sent to me, so what can I take from it?' This will move you away from stuckness and allow you to grow.

Whether you're experiencing a curveball or a moment of joy, reflecting on it from the 'life is happening for me' mindset will yield gifts. It will allow you to see so much more than whatever the event was.

I speak often at events around the world, sharing this mindset with as many people as I can. It is freeing and gives you control; it allows you to take your power back even when the situation may seem dire. This in itself is empowering. You're not being a cork, waiting to see where the tide takes you.

I am sure you can think of many people who have inspired you with how they have overcome apparently disastrous occurrences in their lives. They seem so strong and so courageous, yet all it is, is a mindset. It's thinking differently from how we are programmed.

One person who has really inspired me is a lady named Martine Wright MBE. She was sitting in one of the carriages on a London Tube train when a terrorist's bomb went off on 7 July 2005. Martine lost both her legs.

At the time, she had a young family and worked full time in London. She certainly had someone to blame and could have spent the rest of her life doing just that, resenting the group that planned the bombing.

Martine was filmed for a short documentary where she said that she knew she had to do something as a result of losing her legs that day, otherwise it would have been a complete waste of her life. Focusing on what she could do, she started to play sitting volleyball. She worked at it, trained and qualified to represent Great Britain in the World Championships. She says she feels so lucky to be living this dream, maybe she was meant to wake up late that morning in 2005 and board that particular train. When she looked for the lessons from a 'life is happening for her' mindset, she saw how this event could shape her life.

Martine is someone totally at ease, in control and living from an empowerment mindset.

When a client comes to see me, there's usually been an incubation period. In most cases, the client has been thinking about doing something for around six months. They have procrastinated, distracted themselves, lied to themselves, until eventually they realise the pain is too much to take any longer. Then they book their appointment when the time is right for them. Most can hardly believe that they find a solution in as little as three sessions of pain-free fun and discovery.

You are here at the right time for you. Congratulations.

2
Beliefs Are Both The Truth And An Illusion

I know, you probably feel like you need to read that again. How can this be true? Beliefs are real. They play out, they define us; or at least it seems that way.

That's all an illusion.

In this chapter, we are going to look at what this means for you. What is the handbrake that is holding you back? You may not be able to articulate what this is, but you can feel it.

What exactly is a belief? According to the *Oxford Dictionary of English*, it is:

> '… an acceptance that something exists or is true, especially one without proof.'

I prefer to think of a belief in this way:

What you believe about yourself, you will never surpass.

Even if a belief is limiting, you are being defined by it. You will create a reality that emulates this belief, limiting yourself and potentially those around you.

Where you are in your life right now has been guided by what you believe about yourself; what you believe you can and can't do. This is why beliefs feel so much like the truth. Your filters – what you look for in life – will support your belief structure.

Our filters

Research from Radboud University shows that we are bombarded by approximately 11,200,000 bits of information every second. Our neurology would be totally overloaded if there were no filters to lighten the load of what comes into our system. Imagine 11 million toothpicks being dropped on your head every second. Pretty soon, you would be covered in them and probably pulling them out of your hair for weeks.

The clever thing is that we have around eighteen filters that reduce our 20 million bits to a mere 148 bits per second. That makes our environment so much more manageable, although we have just deleted a lot of 'reality'.

Imagine you go to a party. You have a great time and love the music, the food, the people, the environment. Everything about it works for you.

You notice one of your neighbours at the same party and you say hi. Then a couple of days later, you run into them at the supermarket and talk about how much you loved the party. They reply that they didn't enjoy the party at all and left early. They found the music too loud, the food too spicy and they didn't connect with the people there. What's interesting is you both experienced the same party – same venue, same food, same people. Everything was the same.

If we assume that at the party, 11 million bits of information enter both your neurology and your neighbour's every single second. In essence, this is the actual reality. What happens with your neurological filters is that they whittle the information down to 148 bits every second, so you are each left with an illusion of reality. In fact, it's just your filters giving you a false sense of reality. This is why the same party feels so different to two people who have different filters and delete different pieces of information.

It's important to note that this all happens unconsciously. This means it's out of our conscious awareness. We are blissfully unaware that what we each experience is not the actual reality, just an illusion that it is.

There are three main filters that do the heavy lifting for us so we don't become overwhelmed by the environment. The first one is a deletion filter – it literally deletes data from the environment.

Our deletion filter

I used to travel a lot and developed a little game I would play when I arrived at an airport. You may well have experienced and relate to it yourself. Here's how it works.

How many people on average within a two-hour wait at the airport, when called for their flights, apparently 'push back'? How many are no-shows? On average in my little game, I hear this kind of announcement twice:

'Would Mr and Mrs Longbottom on flight EZY369 bound for Barcelona please make their way immediately to gate 53 where this flight is waiting to depart. Failure to do so will result in your bags being lifted off the aircraft immediately.'

Let's unpack this. Mr and Mrs Longbottom have probably put a lot of effort into the holiday to Barcelona. They've been online and booked their flights with easyJet. These budget aircraft tend to take off early in the morning, so depending on where they live, they may have had to leave the house at 4am for 6am check-in. That's a lot of commitment.

They've clearly arrived at the airport as they've checked their bags in, queued to have them tagged and sent off to the hold. They've gone through security and passport control – which let's face it, nobody really likes – and now they're somewhere in the airside of the airport.

After all the excitement and planning that's gone into this trip, at the last minute, Mr and Mrs Longbottom drop the ball.

What's actually happened here? The Longbottoms' deletion filter has literally deleted the information that's been coming through the tannoy. Most people in the airport have heard it, but Mr and Mrs Longbottom have failed to do so. The deletion filter is operating perfectly.

You will have experienced a deletion filter first-hand. Perhaps you've communicated something to a partner or a child and they've got no recollection of you ever saying whatever it was. They have literally deleted what it was that you said. When you ask your partner if they want a cup of tea while they are looking at something on social media, it may really annoy you when they don't answer you, but it's not because they're being rude; it's because their deletion filter has deleted the information and they haven't heard what you said. Just like Mr and Mrs Longbottom about to miss their flight to Barcelona.

Our distortion filter

The second heavy lifter is our distortion filter. This is where we distort the incoming information to match our own version of reality, which is particularly difficult to manage. It shows up a lot in the workplace – I bet you will have first-hand experience of what I mean.

Imagine you have just had a conversation with a colleague at work and communicated – in your opinion, very clearly – what you need them to do. Then you leave it with them. When you review their actions, they are completely different to those you required from them, the actions you communicated so clearly.

Like your unresponsive partner, your work colleague is not being difficult. It's because they unconsciously distorted the information you communicated to fit their version of reality. Remember the neighbour who didn't enjoy the party you loved?

Another example again involves communicating with one of your children. You tell your child that you want them home by 8.30pm and they arrive home at 9.30pm. They then say that's what you said they could do. All they've done is distort the information you communicated to match their needs. Not great, I know, but as this distortion operates out side the child's conscious awareness, they really aren't being awkward; they are unaware this has happened until they get home at 9.30 and have you to deal with.

We have a saying in our house: the quality of the communication we deliver is shown in the response we get. We all need to be aware that other people's filters will delete and distort what we say to match their reality.

Our generalisation filter

The last heavy lifter is the generalisation filter. We are all used to using this one, albeit outside our conscious awareness. This filter allows us to make sense of the world around us by generalising so it fits with what we know.

For example, how many uses do you think a paperclip has? Most people would think around ten to fifteen, however, Sir Ken Robinson, an expert in education, showed that there are around 200 uses for a paperclip. Kindergarten children are much more creative or divergent in their thinking as they don't yet have a developed generalisation filter. They are not putting a paperclip into a box; they think outside that box. A longitudinal study of kindergarten children measured 98% of children at the genius level of divergent thinking. Five years later when the children were aged eight to ten years, those genius levels had dropped to 50%.

After another five years, the level had dropped further. As time goes by, the generalisation filter is more developed, so divergent thinking deteriorates further. Our world becomes boxed in if we are not careful.

An example of the generalisation filter serving us well comes from my personal experience of hiring a car. I was due to speak at a corporate conference in New Zealand and the organiser sent me an email to say that she'd booked my flights and hired me a car so I could travel to the venue. This car she'd hired was a Hyundai and I've never driven this type of car before, yet my generalisation filter kicked in nicely for me.

If my generalisation filter hadn't done that, I would probably have downloaded the driver's manual for the Hyundai or watched some YouTube videos to understand how to drive this car. All that actually happened was I picked up the car from the airport, programmed the venue details into Google Maps on my phone and off I drove.

We use our generalisation filter all the time to make sense of our world. In the case of this example, it was useful as I could hop into a different make of car to that which I was used to driving and off I went.

Basically, our generalisation filter allows us to say this looks like that, and so we need to respond in that way. It allows us to compare anything out there that may be new to us and generalise it using an experience we've already had. On the whole, it allows us to navigate our world a lot more easily.

The downside of a generalisation filter is that it can limit our learning. Have you ever been researching how to do something online or been on a course and compared what you're reading or hearing to something else you have done before? That's your generalisation filter telling you that you already know how to do it. Your mind can become closed to learning.

These three heavy-lifting filters allow you to make sense of your world and create your reality, so it is good to know that this is only your version of reality and not everyone else's. This is why it is true to say there is no such thing as reality. How can there be when everyone is filtering 11 million bits of information per second down to 148 bits?

Our filters create our reality

A social experiment was run by Carlsberg in Brussels, and I use it in my training courses as it is such a great example of there being no such thing as reality. Imagine the scene. There are 148 bad boys already in a movie theatre, sitting down waiting for the movie to start. There are two seats left in the middle of the theatre.

At the ticket desk outside, an unassuming couple are purchasing two tickets to go and see the same movie. Of course, they've got no idea what they will face when they walk into the theatre.

It's interesting to watch the different reactions depending on the different versions of reality for each couple. Some couples turn and leave immediately. Some couples have a little disagreement, with one of them saying, 'Have you seen those guys?' and the other giggling and saying, 'This looks like fun,' while leading the way to the two seats. As soon as they sit down, the whole theatre gives them a round of applause and passes them two ice-cold Carlsbergs.

The truth is that whatever the couples did became their reality. The ones who left would go on to tell themselves and others that this movie theatre attracts undesirable characters and is best avoided, even if it means driving for two hours to go to watch a movie in the future. The ones who went in will have a different reality.

'You'll never guess what happened the other night,' they'll say to their family and friends. 'It was so cool. We made some really great friends and we got to drink cold beer for free.'

The same environment, the same people, different realities.

How beliefs gain strength

Our filters not only create our reality, they also seek evidence from the world around us to support it, just like our movie goers making snap judgments on the environment they were walking in to. This brings us back to our beliefs and how they shape our reality: they seek evidence to support them. Then when our beliefs deliver the reality we're expecting, we build it into our script, telling people about it and metaphorically rolling our eyes at the evidence backing up what we 'know' to be true.

'This always happens to me,' we say, or, 'Every time I try to… this is what happens.'

What you believe about yourself defines you. It creates your reality. It may feel like the truth, yet it is just an illusion. Now you can see that, knowing what you have learned about filters.

Here's an example of what you believe creating your reality. Have a think about the people who know you the best, those who love you. If I were to ask them what they believe about you, what would they say?

My guess is they would say wonderful things and they would be shocked if you didn't agree with them. Their reality will be different from yours, yet to you, whatever limiting beliefs you are running feel true to you and you work hard at not letting others know what they are.

Some clients tell me they are frightened they will get found out; that if people really knew what they were like, they wouldn't believe it. Clients in high positions in successful organisations tell me they have just got lucky; they don't really know what they are doing and they are hoping they never get caught out.

Some call this imposter syndrome; I call it the illusion syndrome. There is no imposter for the client; it is their truth. At least, that is how it feels.

Yet it is still an illusion.

THERE IS NO SUCH THING AS REALITY

I was working with a client in the UK. Paula was at the top of her game, ran a successful business and was well known for what she did. She had a huge social media following and often appeared on podcasts and YouTube as an influencer.

We were working on what limiting beliefs she was running, uncovering that she thought she was stupid. She was visibly upset by this.

PAULA: Well, that felt bad. Oh my God! This is it, I believe I am stupid.

AMANDA: On a scale of 1 to 10, 1 being I can hardly feel it and 10 being 'Oh, Amanda, this is really true and painful', what number would you give this feeling?

PAULA: It's a 9, it feels true. It *is* the truth.

AMANDA: So you would know if that changed, wouldn't you?

PAULA: Yes.

AMANDA: I know this feels true to you and probably explains a lot for you, yet this is only your version of reality. When I say 'only', please know that what you feel and what you believe to be your truth are hugely important.

PAULA: But this feels like it is the truth for me.

AMANDA: I know. I want to ask you what your best friend would say if I was to share with her what you have just said. Would she say that you are stupid?

PAULA: (laughing) She would say that's rubbish. She would think *you* were stupid for asking her that.

AMANDA: (laughing with Paula) So she would not agree?

PAULA: Hell, no.

Let's look at this. The belief that she is stupid feels true for Paula, but a person who knows and loves her – her best friend – would totally disagree. This is how beliefs are both truth and an illusion, depending on whose filters they are viewed through.

The truth is that we don't see the world as it is; we see the world as we are. Let's read that again.

We don't see the world as it is; we see the world as we are.

How we show up in the world is how we see it. Think back to the movie theatre: those who left saw it as a scary place where they were in danger; those who stayed were curious to watch the movie in a full theatre. It was the same theatre with the same people, yet how it looked to the couples depended on how they saw their 'world'.

LIMITING BELIEFS BOTH DRIVE US AND HOLD US BACK

A client I worked with was the founder of a successful business. Anyone from the outside looking in would say he was talented and confident, yet when we got to the bottom of the limiting belief he was running, it was that he was a failure.

How could this be possible? Surely, he couldn't believe that?

The truth is that he didn't see his world as *it* is; he saw his world as *he* is: a failure. He had been faking it till he made it and he never felt like he had made it, so he worked harder and harder trying to disprove the belief that shook him to his core every day.

The more successful he became, the more he felt like a fraud, yet at some level the limiting belief served him. It drove him. If he lost this drive, then what would happen? Better to ignore the fact the belief was limiting, keep doing what he was doing and faking it.

It is true to say that whatever limiting belief a client is running, it will serve them to a certain extent. It will drive them, but it will also keep them safe, keep them small, stop them from failing so they have no opportunity to learn from mistakes. Its benefits sometimes outweigh the pain that the limiting belief generates, so the client will hold on to it. Sometimes for years. Sometimes for life.

The longer a limiting belief runs in your system, the more powerful it becomes. The belief runs on a neural network, so the more time this fires, the stronger the belief becomes. Think of it as a sharp object running down a piece of wood. Each time you score the wood, the cut becomes deeper and deeper. The same thing happens with a belief. It looks for evidence to back it up from the environment around you and every time it filters that evidence in, it becomes stronger.

I love working with children because their beliefs haven't run for a long time, so they haven't done much damage. The oldest client I have worked with was eighty-three and boy, was she furious when she realised she could have deleted her limiting belief years ago. She couldn't believe how simple it was.

Your world becomes smaller when your limiting belief ripples out into all areas of your life. You lose your self-confidence and self-esteem; think little of yourself; please others to fill the gap. Then symptoms such as anxiety can creep in.

WHY PLEASING OTHERS BEFORE YOURSELF DOESN'T WORK

I was working with Claire, a client who was in her seventies. She had felt less than adequate for much her life. This is how the conversation went:

AMANDA: Tell me specifically what you would like to take from our time together today.

CLAIRE: It's interesting, I don't really know how to answer that. I know that things need to change; I'm just not sure *what* needs to change. I feel that I'm not being myself, although I don't know what that even means.

AMANDA: How do you know that you're not being yourself?

CLAIRE: Now that I'm getting older, I realise that some things are lacking and this has been the case pretty much all my life. I tend to run around and please everybody else before myself, compromising what I really want to make others happy. I guess you could call me a people pleaser, but as I'm getting older, I can see that this is just a pattern. It only allows me to feel fulfilled for a moment.

AMANDA: When was the last time you did something for you, to please you?

CLAIRE: I can't remember. To be honest, if I did, then I would feel guilty about it.

AMANDA: Earlier you said that things haven't been right for some time now. Would you say that things have got worse as you've gotten older?

CLAIRE: I would definitely say things have got worse. As I've got older, I've noticed that I think things about myself that are not good. I talk to myself in a way that is unkind and sometimes I find it really difficult when people are nice to me or pay me a compliment. I believe that they are only being nice to make me feel better.

AMANDA: And does it?

CLAIRE: No, it reminds me of how little I think of myself.

This narrative is typical of older clients that my team and I work with. They have been living from a limiting belief for so long without even realising that it is something they can change. What happens then is that the belief becomes stronger the longer it runs in the client's neurology and the client becomes smaller.

An empowering belief behaves in the same way. When we work with a child who has been given an empowering belief by those around them, we see them grow with that empowering belief, which gets stronger and stronger.

Think of people you know who seem to be confident. They have it all and life just flows to them. They have probably been running core empowering beliefs for some time; they really believe in themselves and others around them. Now think of people who are 'cup half empty' types. Have they always been like this and got worse as they have gotten older?

My team and I work with the Dyslexia Foundation of New Zealand (DFNZ). What's interesting about this work is that we are connecting with people who are aware that they are dyslexic, whether or not they have had a formal diagnosis. The reason that we were invited into this space is because the founders of the DFNZ had done some work with us around belief change. They found this to be an incredible process to allow them to move away from beliefs that were limiting them and step into something that was far more empowering. They even trained with us so they could understand what was going on under the radar.

We have a process called 'Belief Change the Family Journey' in which we support young people who have been diagnosed with dyslexia and people much older who have travelled the dyslexic road with all its bumps and turns. The reason this is called the Family Journey is because it is just that: the whole family is supported, not just the individual, which is so important.

It's true to say that if a child with dyslexia hasn't had a formal diagnosis, they may have already taken on a limiting belief that they are stupid or not good enough. They will have noticed that they are different from their friends; they are struggling. Their limiting belief can manifest itself in different ways, from trying to hide away to being the class clown or resorting to bad behaviour so they're labelled naughty.

A formal diagnosis gives the family the opportunity to take action and look at what they can change. The limiting belief can then be removed. It is hugely empowering to the person who has always thought that they are stupid to know that this belief can change for them. They will also be able to make sense of why things have been the way they have been for them. Then they will see dyslexia in a new light: a superpower, if you like. Life will be happening for them, not to them.

Our role within the DFNZ framework is to address not the literacy issue, but the belief issue. In fact, on the DFNZ website, it says 'Dyslexia's greatest difficulty is self-esteem; it only becomes a disability if not properly addressed'.

Having worked with the DFNZ for the last few years, we've encountered a wide range of ages. It's exciting to work with a young child and help them install an empowering belief such as 'I can do anything I put my mind to.' I will share more about this in Chapter 4; for now, I want to focus on the fact that beliefs left to run pick up strength.

HOW A LIMITING BELIEF CAN GROW

I was working with a client who was in her late sixties. She had been diagnosed with dyslexia many years ago and came to me through the DFNZ, having decided that she wanted to embark on 'Belief Change the Family Journey'. When I asked her what it was that she believed about herself, she was very clear.

'I've always believed I'm stupid, that I'm not able to do what other people can do, and I have believed this all my life. In fact, the older I have got, the more I've believed it. I hide so as not to get caught out, avoid playing games in case people notice how stupid I am. It has become me.'

I asked my client what she tried in the past and she said that she had done a lot of work on herself and had been to personal development courses to improve this low self-esteem issue. Nothing had worked. She would feel better, inspired and motivated in the short term, but eventually this would wear off and she would be back to where she started, or worse.

She noticed she actually felt worse after trying to resolve her self-esteem issues as she thought the reason she hadn't changed was because she was stupid. This backed into the limiting belief once again, giving it more evidence and power.

Why faking it until you make it doesn't work

What have people used in the past to change beliefs that do not serve them? Affirmations. What exactly is an affirmation?

An affirmation is purported to be an empowering statement that a person repeats over and over again, usually out loud, to counter their limiting beliefs. Generally, an affirmation has been written for the person by someone else. When the user of an affirmation has not written it themselves, this is concerning right from the get-go.

You can buy books on affirmations and see them all over social media. Ignore them.

Affirmations are the epitome of faking it till you make it.

The reality is that most people who use affirmations never make it. They give up as each time they say their affirmations out loud (which is generally the recommended course of action), they feel like it's a lie. The affirmation only serves to remind them of the truth they feel and the limiting belief get its way again. It prevails.

Let's imagine that you decide to use affirmations in a way that's in alignment with you. These affirmations are created specifically for you. This is how it would likely play out.

Firstly, you would sit down and write the affirmation you want to have in your life. This affirmation is born from whatever it is that you want to believe about yourself as opposed to what you currently believe about yourself. Let's imagine that the limiting belief is 'I'm not good enough'.

To move away from 'I'm not good enough', you might choose 'I can do anything I put my mind to' as your affirmation. You don't need lots of affirmations; you only need one that cancels out the limiting belief you're wanting to move away from. You repeat this daily out loud with conviction for about two years.

'Two years, Amanda?' you may ask. 'You've got to be kidding me! No wonder affirmations don't work.'

Dr Tad James, the founder of a process called Timeline Therapy™, was featured in a movie called *Beyond Belief* where he shares some research with people who used affirmations to remove a limiting belief and install a new one. It took them about two years of repeating the affirmation many times daily. It's a long road if you're going to choose to use affirmations and there's a much easier, quicker and less risky way. We will get to that in Chapter 9, but there's plenty of essential work to be done beforehand.

The problem with an affirmation is that you don't believe it yet. Each time you say it, you feel as though you're faking it; in other words, you are lying to yourself. What happens then, particularly if you're feeling a little bit low, is the limiting belief will rise up, flex its muscles and tell you this affirmation business is a load of rubbish. Who are you to think you can change?

Dangerous.

Even if you get all the conditions correct and have the right affirmation to cancel the limiting belief out, it's still going to take around two years. Wow, that's a long time, and all that time your limiting belief is still growing in power. The other thing with affirmations is that they don't reveal what the core limiting belief is that you need to move away from. This means that you'll be working with something higher up the belief well (more on this in Chapter 3). The reality is if you can name your limiting belief, then that's not it.

This is why affirmations just don't work. You'll be faking it until you make it, and you won't ever make it as you won't be working on the core limiting belief. Steer clear of them.

Now that we've had a good look at how our filters and beliefs create our reality, and we all have different filters and, as a result, different realities, let's now examine exactly what beliefs are.

3
What A Person Believes Is Just Neural Coding

Think about your beliefs throughout your life. Some of them have changed, right?

Do you remember when you were a child and believed in things like Santa Claus, the tooth fairy or the Easter bunny? These things when you were little felt so real and you believed in them so wholeheartedly that you would get excited on the lead up to Christmas or Easter. When one of your baby teeth fell out, you were enchanted with the prospect of the tooth fairy coming at night, taking your tooth and leaving you a treat of some kind. This was what you had been told would happen, so it became a belief of yours.

Reading this, you probably have memories of what this wholehearted belief felt like for you, but you now know that Santa Claus and the tooth fairy don't exist. That belief is no longer true for you. In the past, you changed your beliefs about things you once felt passionately were an absolute truth for you.

We also have social beliefs of how we should conduct ourselves. Let me give you an example. Imagine you are in a restaurant having dinner with a friend and somebody behind you lights up a cigarette. What would you do?

You'd likely be horrified. This person is not only breaking the law, but also violating something that you believe is true: people should not smoke in public places.

Now let's rewind time back to the early 2000s. If the same thing happened then, what would you do? You might find it annoying, yet you wouldn't have the belief that this is unacceptable.

During the Covid-19 pandemic, we knew that when we went out in public, we needed to wear a face mask. Yet prior to 2020, if somebody had told us that we would believe it to be true that we must always have a mask with us, we would probably not have believed them.

Our beliefs change with time, often without us realising it. It happens under the radar and it takes time.

We can change what we believe because all beliefs are just neural coding – information processed by our neurons. Given that we can change what we believe about things external to us, we can also change our beliefs at our core. With this in mind, I have something to ask you.

An important question for you

If you could believe anything about yourself without fail, what would that be?

Whatever you truly believe about yourself, you will become. In fact, I'd go as far as to say that you will never surpass what you truly believe about yourself.

In many respects, the only thing that's holding you back is what you truly believe. Knowing now that this can be changed, what belief would serve you better?

When my team and I work with clients, one of the things we do is ask them to consider this important question. At first, they tend to name the opposite of the belief they're wanting to move away from. That's the general starting place. For example, if the limiting belief is 'I'm not good enough', the answer to the question will be 'I am good enough'.

We then ask them to think big. When they install a new empowering belief, it will be with them for life, so they may as well go for gold and give it all they've got.

Some of the empowering beliefs that clients have installed are:

- I am fucking awesome

- I can do anything I put my mind to

- I am uniquely special

- I am *me*

Even though these are common empowering beliefs, it is important to notice that to each person, they mean different things. One young man even installed 'I am superman' to mean he was capable of anything. I did check whether he intended to take up flying and wearing underpants over his jeans, to which he laughed.

Whatever your answer to the question, it will give you an idea of the limiting belief you are wanting to move away from. Sometimes, all we can see are the symptoms of our limiting belief. You will be able to name the symptoms of the limiting belief; you will be able to feel how these show up in your life on a daily basis driven by the limiting belief. It's probably one of the reasons why you picked up this book: you're trying to move away from these symptoms.

These are some of the symptoms that the clients my team and I work with talk about:

- I lack confidence.

- I hate going to a social function on my own.

- I never seem to finish anything.

- I don't like to have to talk in front of people.

- I run around trying to please others.

- I compromise my happiness.

- I think I don't have much to offer.

- If people knew what I was really like, they wouldn't believe it.

These are symptoms because they are the effects of the limiting belief; they are not the cause. Notice that none of these are 'I am' statements. Core limiting beliefs usually start with 'I am...' and whatever follows will define you.

Now you have connected with the symptoms of your limiting belief, you don't even need to list them. You can feel them, give them a nod – 'Yes, I know you are there.' They will feel familiar.

Here's my next question.

What is your limiting belief?

Have a go. What do you think it might be?

My team and I always encourage our clients to go to the bottom of the well to get right to the core of their limiting belief structure. Here's why.

Beliefs have a hierarchy, which is why we talk about a well. The deeper down the well we go, the more weight and power the limiting belief we find has.

Think of a limiting belief that operates at the core of you being a little like a weed in your garden. Your aim is to pull the weed up from the roots, rather than cutting the weed down bit by bit and saving the root until last. Then the whole weed comes out of the ground.

You want a deep deletion of the core limiting belief, the one that is going to give you the best bang for your buck rather than you having to come back week after week to hack at the weed. It takes courage to go that deep.

EXPLORING THE DEPTHS OF THE WELL

I worked with a client in the United States called Kaihan Krippendorff, a best-selling author of five books and a global speaker, who was referred to me. He told me he wanted a belief change around his skills in business. We worked on his limiting belief, deleted it and installed another belief that would better serve him.

After around six months, he came back for another belief change deeper down the well. About four months later, he came again, then again, each time going deeper until we got to the core.

Then boom! He got it. He realised that if he had gone deep right at the beginning, he would have pulled the metaphorical weed out from the roots. It would have been much quicker and more cost effective.

Being as resourceful as he is, though, he decided to write his fifth book called *Driving Innovation From Within* and dedicated a chapter to belief change. He asked me to co-write this with him.

Kaihan loves the belief-change process. What he believed about himself was just neural coding; it was not personal. It was not Voodoo or mystical; it was just a neural network that could be deleted.

Kaihan's book is listed in the Further Resources section at the back for you.

Here are the top limiting beliefs my team and I work with on a regular basis:

- I am not good enough.

- I am not smart enough.

- I am not a nice person.

- I am not loveable.

- I am unworthy.

- I am a mistake.

- I am broken.

- I am not enough.

- I hate myself.

As you read through them, you may have felt drawn towards some statements more than others as being true for you. The wording might not be exactly right for you, but the essence of the belief connected with you.

If you were to have a guess, what would you say is your limiting belief? How does this show up in your life? Once you have an idea, just knowing that is powerful.

When I am working with a client, they often can't name their limiting belief as it runs outside of conscious awareness. It is under the radar, so it is the unthinkable. What we start with in this case are the symptoms: how the limiting belief affects them daily. I call this the 'drop-down menu' of the limiting belief.

For the moment, let's leave the limiting belief as a blank title. Underneath that is the drop-down menu: the symptoms. It's easier to connect with the symptoms rather than the limiting belief because the client can name them – that's why they came to see me in the first place. The symptoms are causing them pain, so they know what they are; what they don't realise is that there is a deeper source that drives all these symptoms.

PINPOINTING A LIMITING BELIEF

Here's how Sally, a client of mine, recognised what symptoms – behaviours in her daily life – her limiting belief created for her.

AMANDA: Tell me, what is the biggest thing for you that, if it changed today, would change you?

SALLY: To stop self-sabotaging. I do it all the time; I have this voice that puts me down.

AMANDA: Who's voice is it?

SALLY: That's funny, I never thought of that before. It's my voice.

AMANDA: What is it saying to you?

SALLY: That I can't do it, or who do I think I am? It sounds silly when I say it out loud, but it's true.

AMANDA: How else do you self-sabotage?

SALLY: I keep myself small. Like, I was invited to go to a work function. It was an evening do and I knew it would be a good thing to go, but I backed out; I said I was not well. I just hated the idea of walking into the room by myself and having to chat to people. I mean, what was I going to say to them? I am so boring.

In this short narrative, we can see the symptoms and how they showed up in this client's life. This was a real problem for her and, as we have already learned, it would only get worse if left unchecked. Sally thought the issue was the self-sabotage. This was what she could feel, but when we looked at what was going on for her from a belief structure and got to the bottom of the well, the root of the weed, the limiting belief was 'I am not worthy'.

When we uncovered this, Sally said it made perfect sense to her. In fact, she told me that the happier she was, the more she sabotaged that happiness because at her core, she was never going to be worthy of it.

This awareness is powerful. It leads to belief change. Sally's life certainly changed.

A limiting belief is only a neural network, but this network will get stronger as time goes on. The symptoms will amplify and the belief will gain more power.

If this has made you think and curious to find out more about your core limiting belief, good. This takes courage.

If you are tempted to put the book down, then this is also feedback. It means you realise you are on a journey of self-discovery and this is scary. You might for the first time understand what it is that has been holding you back. It takes some bravery; it takes some discomfort to confront that.

Are you ready to take a look at the roots of your core limiting beliefs? Let's go there.

4

It's Not Your Fault

At some level, the reason that most of my clients take a long time to come and do change work is because they feel guilty. They feel as though their issues are all their fault. They feel embarrassed because the person who's going to help them make the changes will be aware of what they feel they're responsible for.

Some clients know that their issues are related to their past. When I explain how beliefs are installed into our neurology, they see that this really is not their fault. A limiting belief is no different to an empowering belief in terms of how it is stored and runs in our neurology. The main difference is the outcomes that each one creates.

Interestingly, most limiting beliefs are not at all logical. They make no sense and will often seem totally silly to anyone close to the person running the limiting belief.

How beliefs are installed

Before a child reaches the age of seven, they are learning machines and operate in a hypnotic state. Their brains function in theta, which allows them to absorb so much information from their environment. They are literally little sponges; there is no brain functioning at beta level, which is our conscious mind's way of operating.

Our twin boys are just three years old. They are attending a Portuguese kindergarten where no English is spoken, but they absorb Portuguese far more quickly than Sarah and I would. As a result, they will be bilingual.

Until the age of seven, a child treats everything as a truth. They have no objectivity or ability to disagree as there's no logical thinking in place. There's no judgment or disagreement. If a child is told by a care giver that they are being stupid, then the child's unconscious mind takes this as being a truth. What happens then is the child looks at life through the lens of being stupid and picks up from the environment anything that reflects or confirms that. It's also true to say that the child will delete or put down to being lucky anything that disproves the belief that they're stupid, such as getting an answer correct in class.

I had a client who believed she was stupid, yet she was a medical doctor working in a top London hospital. When I asked her how she had managed to graduate and land this dream job, she told me it was because of her looks. It seems crazy, right? However, it felt real and true for the client. In turn, her behaviour reflected the limiting belief, making it even more real to her. She told me it was only a matter of time until her colleagues at the hospital realised she was stupid.

People's deletion filter will delete anything that doesn't back into their limiting belief. A limiting belief about not being worthy, for example, results in them not being able to take a compliment, thinking that other people are just being 'nice'.

A child will take on belief systems from their parents and close network through the language and behaviour surrounding them. Like a sponge, they absorb everything. Dove, the body-care brand, did a social experiment on this a few years back. In the experiment, Dove researchers asked mothers what they disliked about their bodies. The mothers wrote a list.

The researchers then asked the daughters, who were all around the age of six, the same question. What was both interesting and disturbing was the daughters' lists were almost identical to the mothers'. In fact, the daughters' wording around their body image was the same as the mothers'.

For example, one mother wrote down that she liked her legs because they were good for running. Her daughter wrote the exact same thing. Another said she didn't like her eyes because they were small. Her daughter wrote down the same words. They had adopted the same beliefs as their mums, whether they be positive or negative, once again highlighting the point that the unconscious mind has no judgment. It takes in information as a truth, then looks for the evidence to support it, reinforcing the neural network and belief each and every time.

No decent parent knowingly installs limiting beliefs into their child, but all beliefs are installed the same way. However, some are much more harmful than others, such as those on the list you'll have read in the What is your limiting belief? section earlier in this chapter. In fact, I have never worked with a client on a limiting belief about body image; this is very much at the top of the well.

If a child has a positive environment, people who inspire and challenge them, support them and use language that empowers rather than limits them, then they have a much better chance of having empowering beliefs at their core for life. One example is Richard Branson. Eve, his mum, would drive him to his grannie's house, which was around three miles away. Richard was being naughty in the back seat so she stopped the car half way and told Richard to make his own way on foot. He was six years old.

He would knock on doors, ask for water, ask for directions. This way, he learned that people wanted to help him, that people are inherently good. He now runs around 400 companies and is the king of delegation, which he puts down to his early exposure to finding and trusting people who can do things better than he can. What Eve did for him at that tender age was install an empowering belief that people can be trusted, people will help. You can take a look at a short letter that Richard made for Eve after she passed away where he thanks her for all she did in raising him, the link is in the resources section.

Another example I use when I am presenting at a DFNZ workshop is that of Thomas Edison. Allegedly, Thomas was seven when he came home from school with a sealed letter and handed it to his mother, Nancy. Thomas asked what the letter said; Nancy opened it and read it aloud.

'Your son is a genius. This school is too small for him and doesn't have good enough teachers to train him. Please teach him yourself.'

Many years later, Thomas was going through his mum's personal things after she passed away and found the letter in a box. This time, he read it for himself.

'Your son is mentally deficient. We cannot let him attend our school anymore. He is expelled.'

Thomas later said, 'My mother was the making of me. She was so true and so sure of me, I felt that I had someone to live for, someone I must not disappoint.'

Neither Richard nor Thomas had a choice in the empowering beliefs that were installed in their unconscious mind before their conscious mind had a chance to question anything. The same is true for you. You did not have a say in the beliefs that were installed in you, be they empowering or limiting. It is not your fault and there's no merit in trying to decipher whose fault it is.

When clients try to identify who installed the limiting belief they are running, I encourage them not to spend time looking at this. It doesn't serve a useful purpose; all it does is keep the client stuck. What's helpful to consider is that the person would not have done this intentionally. People generally don't know how belief systems are installed; they are doing the best they can with the resources they have at that moment.

SUPERMARKET FRUSTRATIONS

We've established that the unconscious mind takes everything personally, it takes everything literally. What does that actually look like in real life?

Let's imagine you've taken your small child to the supermarket. You've got a lot on your mind, particularly around finances, and your child is not really enjoying the trip to the supermarket, until they see a toy that they want. They ask for the toy repeatedly as only a small child can. Each time, you gently say no, not today, but the child's persistent and you're getting more and more irritable.

Then you finally find yourself saying they can't have a toy because they haven't been good enough. It might be that they've frustrated you, they've cried or wittered, so you use your get-out-of-jail card to stop them from going on about the toy.

What happens in the child's neurology, though, is this. The child thinks, 'OK, I'm not good enough and that's why I can't have the toy.' Then the unconscious mind goes out into the environment to find evidence to support the belief, newly reinstalled in the child, that 'I'm not good enough'. Each time they find examples of where they've fallen short – and they will find them – that belief gets stronger and stronger as the neural network is fired again and again.

When your child is older than seven, their conscious processing kicks in. They have a gatekeeper; they can make 'sense' of the situation. Basically, their brains are functioning at beta level, so they are able to rationalise what is going on. This child would ask once, maybe twice, and then realise through the thinking logical brain that this is a no go right now and it's best to ask later when you're more relaxed and in a better mood. Even though you've said no, the child's taking that on board and realising there's a different way to get the outcome that they want.

Now that you know, I'm sure you'll be mindful around the little ones in your life, ensuring that you're protecting their neurology from harmful belief systems. It is true to say that every time we open our mouths, we are influencing those around us, and every time we listen, we are being influenced. You will likely be thinking about the children around you who are not yet seven and those who are older. You might find yourself curious about who was responsible for influencing your mind when you were a child. Let it go.

Let's focus on what you can control.

Installing empowering beliefs in our children

Sarah and I decided to try an experiment with our babies when they were in utero. We did some research around when would be a good time to introduce language and play sounds to them. Three months was the answer.

I created an eight-minute-long hypnosis. I have a Doctorate in Clinical Hypnotherapy, so knew what was needed to create something that we felt would be perfect.

What we wanted to do was install empowering beliefs into the babies right from the start. Sarah and I, along with our team, looked at the common empowering beliefs that we have worked with in our client sessions, much like the list of limiting beliefs you have already read, and developed this list:

- You are kind.

- You are intelligent.

- You have all you need inside of you.

- You are happy.

- You are safe and secure.

- You are loveable.

- Mummy and I love you very much.

This was recorded on a loop with all the lovely sounds and effects that we can create with a bespoke hypnosis recording. We played this every day to them. After a month, we noticed that when we had played the recording, there was increased activity from the babies in utero with lots of kicking and movement.

Then they were born, our beautiful twin boys, and we continued, this time with our own voices, soft and soothing, same words, every day. They liked it; they smiled for the first time when we spoke the list of empowering beliefs for them.

When one of our team, Elli, was staying with Sarah and me, she heard us saying our empowering beliefs list to the boys, who were by then four months old. One afternoon, she looked after them and decided to try it out herself. She used the same words on repeat, but spoken with an Irish accent.

She took a video as she did it. The boys wriggled, smiled, laughed and responded so positively that we realised that it was the words that were familiar to them. They were responding the same way with Elli as they had done with us. They are now three years old. We continue to do this every day and they still love it.

Knowing what we know about how beliefs are installed, we can have confidence that our boys will enjoy these empowering beliefs for life. The neural networks have been set up, so they will fire each and every time the boys' beliefs find the evidence to support them. Powerful.

I share this example whenever I speak as the keynote at a corporate event or training course, even at interviews. In fact, anytime I speak, if I can, I share this.

I would rather give people a workable tool to help their children than work at deleting limiting beliefs later in life.

Sarah and I call this the Empowering Belief Installer. Quite simply, it is how we as parents can install empowering beliefs in our little people.

PREVENTION IS BETTER THAN CURE

After I had been sharing this method for a while, we started to get emails from people who were running the Empowering Belief Installer with their little ones. They told us that the little ones really enjoyed it.

One single mum said it had been a big game changer for her as the only time she really got to tell her son that she loved him was at bedtime. She felt most of the time, she was asking him or nagging him to do things and the 'I love you' at bedtime was becoming white noise. She loved being able to share with him empowering beliefs that she knew were allowing him to become a better person.

What most parents told us was that their children would ask them to say the Empowering Belief Installer. After about a week, the children would start to hand select their own empowering beliefs to say back to their parents, bringing tears to the parents' eyes.

Another thing parents noticed was the children would put symbols to the wording, for example a love heart for 'you are loveable' and a smiley face for 'you are happy'. They would also hold their bodies for 'you are safe and secure'.

I want to make it clear that parents can create their own empowering belief list; it doesn't need to be the one Sarah and I use. What we notice, though, is that our list covers a lot of the main touch points, so most parents run with it.

Then we get the question, which you are likely to be asking too: 'What about children who are older than seven?'

I hear you. When I talk about this subject, I can see from the audience's reaction that parents and grandparents are reeling inside, wondering what they have done to their children.

If that resonates with you, relax. Here's what to do.

Either create your own list or use ours, or use a combination of the two. When your older children are asleep, after forty-five minutes or so, pop into their bedroom. In their left ear, repeat the list three times using a quiet, slow and gentle voice. Then leave.

There's a process called sleep talk, which describes parents doing just this. The unconscious mind is always listening. The gatekeeper, which is the conscious mind, is out to lunch, so you can bypass that and communicate directly with the unconscious mind. This is what makes sleep talk different from affirmations: these don't bypass the conscious mind. This was developed by Joane Goulding and the link for this is in the resource section.

What a person believes about themselves, they will never surpass. Give the young ones in your life the best chance.

If your children are already grown up, whatever limiting beliefs they may have, it's not your fault. It doesn't matter who it was who installed them, they didn't do this on purpose; they were just doing the best they could with the resources they had. Now you have better resources.

It's time to turn the focus back on to the beliefs that are holding you back. What can you do about them?

5

You May Feel Uncomfortable For A While

In my practice in New Zealand, we have a glass door. On it we have a huge circle that says, 'The Changing Room'. Inside the circle, it says 'Change always comes bearing gifts'.

First, though, the client may need to feel some discomfort. They may need to feel a little out of their depth and learn to be comfortable within the discomfort.

Leaning into your discomfort

Change is easy once you grasp the fact it comes with a level of discomfort, but this discomfort is only temporary. It is just you connecting with the pain so you can know how to move away from it.

CONNECTING WITH THE PAIN

This is how connecting with the pain sounded in practice for a client, Sam.

AMANDA: What do you specifically want out of our time together today?

SAM: I am not sure; I just don't want to feel so down. I wake up and already it is a bad day.

AMANDA: OK, so if you don't want to feel down, what do you want to feel instead?

SAM: I am not sure, just not to feel this way.

This is the problem: like Sam, most clients are able to tell my team and me what they don't want yet, but have no insight into what they would rather have. They have never been able to even think about what life would be like if they no longer had the problem because they are so connected to the problem that they are in. They know it so well; it is familiar. Trying to think beyond the familiar is hard.

Perhaps what you have tried in the past to help you change has not had a level of discomfort. It has felt familiar and safe – not that I am suggesting you should ever feel unsafe. It is the comfort that is the issue here. When you are in your comfort zone, learnings and change elude you.

You may have felt a level of discomfort already while reading this book. I mentioned in Chapter 3 that maybe you wanted to put the book down as its content was making your feel uneasy. This is a tell-tale sign you're on the right path to uncovering whatever is holding you back.

Sometimes it is easier to pretend everything is OK. It is easier to pretend everything is good and distract ourselves from what is really going on. Instead, we need to look for the signs of discomfort and press on through. Here's why.

I flew to London from Portugal in 2005 for my first NLP course. I spent time away from home, paid for the course and hotel accommodation and learned the tools.

There was a guy on our course who had simply come along to learn how to help people stop smoking. Back in 2005, the smoking in public places ban was about to be activated in the UK. This guy had no interest in digging deep and sorting any issues out for himself; he only wanted the certification to sell his stop-smoking packages.

The trainer failed him because he was playing along, sabotaging his fellow students' experience of the training and devaluing it by making up problems. Clients don't make up problems; they are very real. To get real change, they need to get uncomfortable and do some digging around to take the weed out by the root.

I currently have twenty-five people in my team, and we are growing. I meet regularly with each team member for development, accountability, support and so we can both work on ourselves as we know we are a work in progress. In other words, we make sure we feel uncomfortable on a regular basis. It's what growth looks like.

Honesty and openness make the difference. We need to be honest with ourselves about what we think we need to change and be prepared to dig deep to uncover the unspeakable: the things that run beneath the surface. This is where the true change happens.

Prepare to feel a little uncomfortable for a while. This is the power that you have; it's where all change happens in the unconscious part of your neurology.

The unconscious mind in action

Let's try a little experiment. Put the book down. Yes, just pop it down close to you so you can still read it, but have your arms free. Done that? Good.

Now fold your arms. Easy, right? You automatically know how you fold your arms.

Unfold your arms and put them down by your side. Give them a little shake. Now fold them the opposite way around.

Hmm, that wasn't so easy, was it? This is because the first time I asked you to fold your arms, you folded them in a way that's comfortable for you; the way that you've been doing it for years. This experience is housed in the unconscious part of your neurology, out of conscious awareness. You didn't have to think about how to fold your arms; you just did it.

What happened when I asked you to fold them the opposite way around was you had to bring this action into conscious awareness. You became aware of what actions were needed to fold your arms.

This simple exercise illustrates something far more powerful: where all change, learning and behaviour is housed. That is in the unconscious mind.

The reason that we feel uncomfortable when real change happens is because we must go on a journey of discovery into the unconscious. This means we don't consciously know what that change will mean for us yet. As I said in Chapter 2, if you can name your limiting belief, that's probably not it. It's not the root of the weed.

What you think you need to work on is only what is shown at the conscious level, the symptoms. According to developmental biologist Dr Bruce Lipton, 95% of our daily behaviours come from the unconscious mind, not the conscious. In other words, we are running on auto-pilot. This is where the change needs to take place.

DISCOMFORT EQUALS GROWTH

A student called Sharron Beardsley joined my team and me for a nine-day course in New Zealand. She came from a corporate background and was used to being able to make lots of notes using highlighter pens whenever she was learning new things. She was most definitely used to having a table in front of her.

When we run our training courses, there are no desks or anything to lean on to make copious amounts of notes. Sharron became concerned because she wasn't able to do what she felt she needed to do to learn in the way she was accustomed to. It took her a few days to relax and get into a new way of learning for her, which was to have fun, absorb, listen, feel uncomfortable.

As we know from the previous chapter, this is how children learn: they absorb information from their environment. Think about a child learning to walk: they watch the adults and older children around them, and then give it a go. They keep trying until they master the skill. We don't see an eighteen-year-old crawling into the room on all fours, saying, 'I never really got that walking thing when I was younger; I just gave up.'

Learning is something we do habitually, but when we become adults, we tend to think it is difficult. Sharron struggled initially as she carried a limiting belief that she was stupid, so learning differently felt risky. She has since gone on to do further education with us and become a part of our team, helping others to make changes.

She remembers fondly the day when she realised there were no desks to learn at. She now can't believe she thought that was the only way she was capable of learning well.

True learning only takes place when discomfort is present, but you need to feel safe about embracing that discomfort and curious about what the journey ahead might be. What happens once the change has taken place? What do you experience and how does that change show up in your life?

What does change look like?

Have you made a change to yourself that has had a tangible impact for the better on how you have lived your life and the decisions that you've made? If you have, then you'll know that this kind of change is literally life changing.

What I aim for with every client is that they receive such a profound, unimaginable change, their life literally transforms. What happens as this starts to show up for the client? Let's take a look.

A belief change takes around thirty minutes, but there is work to be done before the process starts. First, we need to identify what the client's core limiting belief is to make sure that we are working with the correct one. Once this is done, the thirty-minute process is easy. It's literally just the client imagining internal pictures, sounds and feelings. We then play around with those.

For the client, the results are instantaneous, to the point where around 50% of them can't even remember the limiting belief that they had felt so intensely for a long time. While the other 50% can remember the wording of the limiting belief, they no longer feel any of the negative emotions that were connected to it. The change is tangible and it's instant.

When my team and I ask the client to observe their life over the next forty-eight hours, we describe the change as being a little like a new jacket. You notice it the first few times you wear it, and then after you've worn it a few times, it becomes a part of your wardrobe. You put it on and don't think about it again.

The same is true of a belief change. You'll notice it the first time you look through different lenses. Your responses, your thoughts, your actions will all be different. Then it becomes part of your normal life.

My team and I call this forty-eight hour observation period our clients' reality check. Have things changed enough for the client? They always have. This stuff works. It is powerful.

A CLIENT'S REALITY CHECK

Here's what a client said after a belief change with Sarah.

'I was talking to a friend on the phone and telling them about my constant anxiety and how I had lost all my confidence. Generally, I felt so unhappy and cried a lot. I blamed this on numerous things, especially the menopause.

'My friend recommended your company, saying I'd have to dig really deep and give it my all. I have to admit I was sceptical, partly because I was constantly negative about everything and I wondered how anyone was going to help me with a lifelong problem.

'Sarah and I only had two Zoom meetings and wow! What a difference it has made to my life. I don't know how to explain how we did it, but it has been life changing for me. Sarah gave me the tools to stop my anxiety and self-loathing. I don't hate myself and I feel worthy again. I find myself singing all the time and feeling an overall happiness that was missing for so long. The cloud has lifted; the sadness has gone. This change has given me back a good quality of life that I know I deserve.'

When a limiting belief is first installed in the neurology, it takes up a neural network. The more evidence this network finds to support the limiting belief, the stronger it becomes. The same is true of a newly installed empowering belief. This is why my team and I encourage clients to get back to us when they've been living with their new empowering belief for a while.

It doesn't matter how empowering a belief is, it is just a neural network. It works in the same way as a limiting belief. It is not personal; it is not conscious. Once a new empowering belief is installed, it goes about doing its thing and you won't need to consciously activate it. The conscious mind has no place here. You can just relax in the knowledge that all is good and enjoy the benefits of empowerment.

6

Beliefs Are Both Changeable And Permanent

The great thing about beliefs is you have a choice. You can literally delete and install what you like. It's a little like going to the pick and mix when you were a child.

Think about this for a moment. What you thought was permanent is an illusion. Part of you that you felt was who you are can be changed. You didn't even get to choose this part; it was installed without your permission, when you were a child.

The people responsible for installing the belief systems that you are currently running didn't realise they could do that. The beliefs that anyone runs, be they limiting or empowering, are really down to chance.

They depend on your environment when you were young and the people of influence in that environment.

You can choose empowerment

Having worked in the field of belief change since 2005, I find it upsetting that people live from limiting beliefs because they don't realise they have a choice. They have no idea because the beliefs that are running and designing their reality daily feel so real to them. It seems impossible to change a limiting belief, so it feels permanent.

WHAT YOU BELIEVE ABOUT YOURSELF WILL FEEL PERMANENT

When I'm working with a client and they realise that they have a choice and can choose a belief that is going to serve them, this is great. The proof that they are operating from a limiting belief is that they're unable to choose a new belief that's big and compelling. This is the limiting belief showing up and restricting their ability to believe anything different about themselves. They feel as though they have to fake it until they make and pretend that they can have a new empowering belief.

Here's what this looked like for one client, Bruce.

AMANDA: Now that we have identified your limiting belief is 'I'm not good enough', what would you rather believe about yourself?

BRUCE: That's a good question. I never really thought about that before, but I guess it will be to believe that I am good enough.

AMANDA: OK, let's take that as a starting point. The new empowering belief is going to be 'I am good enough'. Does that sound big enough for you? Just say this to yourself and notice how it feels inside.

BRUCE: It feels OK, but I get what you mean by it's not really big enough. I'm not sure what it is that I really want to believe. Can you help me?

The problem here is that Bruce is thinking and behaving from the limiting belief, 'I'm not good enough'. To create something much more empowering means he doesn't feel comfortable. It feels alien to him.

We had to approach this slightly differently and allow Bruce to get really creative about what he would rather believe. I call this the design stage.

This is where it takes courage. You need to find the ability to get out of your comfort zone and go on a journey of self-discovery into the world of the unconscious mind. This will feel as though you are making things up and it is totally fake.

Take this as feedback: this is your limiting belief showing up, tapping you on the shoulder and saying, 'You can't do that, it's not you. This is you, the real you, right here.' Thank your limiting belief for all it has done for you. Have gratitude around it and smile.

This in itself is powerful: it is an awakening, a step further down the path of your biggest self-discovery.

With limiting beliefs, there is something happening in your body physically as well as in your mind. This is called cell inertia. Your cells have become so used to their environment, they adapt to it.

Your neurotransmitters are listening all the time, eavesdropping on your thoughts and taking them as being real. Every thought produces a chemical, a hormone. Dopamine, oxytocin and serotonin produce a happy, upbeat and positive state, while cortisol and adrenaline do the opposite: they produce stress and fear. If you have been used to flooding your cells with cortisol and adrenaline, they will have adapted accordingly. It doesn't matter to them whether this is a good environment. They don't judge it; they just adapt to survive.

Imagine it like this. Your cells are like someone who has become used to the cold winter weather. They have all the gear to survive this as they are used to it, so they have hats and scarves, gloves and hot water bottles. They know the landscape.

This is the cortisol and adrenaline territory. When you try to imagine what your new empowering belief might be, cell inertia holds you back as it's not equipped for this territory. It literally blinds you to the choices you have. This is when beliefs feel permanent and unchangeable. You've got so used to the territory, why change it now? You've got all the gear to live with it.

This is why faking it till you make it doesn't work. When you try to fake it till you make it, it is like taking your cells from the landscape they have been used to living in, the one that they have adapted to, and saying, 'OK, you lot, time to get your swimmers on. We are heading to the sunny climes, so get that sunscreen out.' They are not primed for it and don't know this landscape, so it's not just about saying that things are changing. It's not about affirmations or willpower; you need to change at a neurological and cellular level.

A belief change

I was bad at maths at secondary school. I was in the bottom set and it took me three attempts to pass my maths O level. I believed I was rubbish at maths and the evidence I collected proved that to be true.

I then got a job with a major cosmetic company, working on the customer-facing counter. I needed to know my numbers if I was going to fly through the ranks, but I didn't know where to start.

One of my colleagues was good at numbers, so I shared with her that I was rubbish with them. She helped me understand what to do, but it took a long time and even when I did know what I needed to do, underneath the surface, I still believed that I was rubbish at maths.

This is a classic example of cell inertia. My landscape hadn't changed; my thoughts were still producing the same feelings. Even though I sailed through the scented ranks of the corporation, became the youngest executive to be promoted out of store and hit my targets month after month, I put this down to luck. I had all this success, but my limiting belief was that I was still rubbish at numbers.

Then, in 2005, I found NLP.

At the age of thirty-eight, I deleted the limiting belief that I was rubbish at numbers. For twenty-seven years, I'd had cell inertia that had adapted to this belief, this environment. As much as I wanted to believe I was good with numbers, the cell inertia wasn't equipped for this environment and the limiting belief continued to tell me that fundamentally, that was a lie.

Deleting the limiting belief was liberating. Had I not come across belief change, I would still be shying away from numbers, and I can assure you that would not have been a good thing.

When my late husband Keith was alive, he did all the numbers in our home and looked after all our finances. Then during his last week earth side, he gave me a crash course on how our finances worked, what I needed to do and how I needed to do it. As well as dealing with the pain of him leaving, I also had to buckle down and learn the household numbers, but believing that I was infinitely capable allowed me just to get on with it. If I had been running the old belief, I would have been overwhelmed like a rabbit caught in the proverbial car headlights.

My belief change saved me, and yet I waited twenty-seven years to be free of it. Can your belief change save you? Are you prepared to look at what is going on for you that is holding you back; look at your cell inertia and change the landscape? What will your life be like if you don't want to go there? If you stay the same and think you're not able to step into this?

A glimpse into the future

If you are curious, let's play a game. You can dive straight into this now or come back to it; your call. It will work much better if you are alone, can speak out loud and are relaxed as this game may feel uncomfortable. In fact, it should make you feel uncomfortable.

Are you happy to be in discomfort for a small amount of time to find out what your life could be like? Yes? You want get into it now?

OK, let's go.

Say out loud (or inside if you prefer, but out loud is more effective) what your limiting belief is, or at least what you think it is for now. I can assure you, whatever you say is probably not the root of the weed; it will likely be something higher up the well, but it will still give you great information.

Now feel the emotional costs this belief has had on your life. Connect with your symptoms. How has this limiting belief affected your relationships, physical body, spiritual body and level of happiness? Answer out loud if possible; say whatever comes to your mind.

What do you regret most because of this belief? Again, out loud.

Now imagine that you have moved two years into the future and dragged this limiting belief with you. Notice everyone around you is two years older. The belief itself is two years older and has more power, while other things have moved on. People have moved on.

Again, feel the emotional costs this belief has had on your life. How has this limiting belief affected your relationships, your physical body, your spiritual body and your level of happiness? Say it out loud.

What do you regret most because of having this belief? Again, out loud.

Now, imagine you have moved five years into the future and dragged this limiting belief with you. Everyone around you is five years older; the belief is five years stronger. Feel the emotional costs this belief has had on your life. How has it affected your relationships, physical body, spiritual body and level of happiness?

What do you regret most because of this belief? Say it out loud.

Finally, repeat the process while imagining that you have moved ten years into your future and dragged this limiting belief with you. It may be hard, but say the answers to the questions out loud. What do you regret most because of having this belief?

Recognise that none of this has happened yet. Your unconscious mind has given you a glimpse of what your future could hold if you continue to live with that limiting belief. You have the chance to change it.

Your unconscious mind is designed to seek wholeness. It does not want anything for you that will not create wholeness, and what you have probably just experienced does not create that. You have a choice. What would you rather believe?

One last time, say this out loud.

You may have found this painful; it may have been insightful. It is interesting to look at yourself ten years from now and imagine what life might be like if you stay the same.

This is great information for you. You've had the chance to see the future before it's happened. You have seen what might happen if you do nothing. This is a gift: you now know something can be done about it.

Go big. What would help you to live your best life? What belief would take you there? If you could truly believe this about yourself, what would life be like? How would this belief show up in your day-to-day life? How would you know it is showing up?

For me, this was being able to get on with the numbers, not second guessing myself. I could look forward to planning and make wise choices, just as Keith had done.

Remember the drop-down menu of symptoms of limiting beliefs we looked at in Chapter 3? It's the same for an empowering belief: there's a drop-down menu of symptoms that prove this belief is showing up in your life.

Let's take a look at several clients' empowering beliefs and drop-down menus of symptoms. This will give you some ideas and insights as to how this all works.

Limiting belief: 'I am a horrible person'.

Empowering belief: 'I am an incredible person'.

Drop-down menu:

- I am strong.
- I am kind.
- I can do anything I put my mind to.
- I am fun.
- I am a good friend.
- I fit in everywhere.
- I am *enough*.
- I am intelligent.
- I am loved.
- I am beautiful.
- I love me.
- I am amazing.

Limiting belief: 'I am a mistake'.

Empowering belief: 'I am magical'.

Drop-down menu:

- I do amazing things.
- I am capable of doing *anything* I put my mind to.

- I am loved.

- I am loving.

- I am kind.

- I am wisdom filled.

- I am me and love me.

Limiting belief: 'I am dirty'.

Empowering belief: 'I am worthwhile and deserving'.

Drop-down menu:

- I am caring.

- I am happy and healthy.

- I am positive.

- I have stickability.

- I can do anything.

- I am happy.

- I am loved.

- I love myself.

This is a quote from one client who did this work:

> 'My mind is "light", but full of hope for what my future holds for my husband and me. I am

finding it difficult to describe the feelings I am experiencing with this huge shift. The one that I truly can name is huge gratitude to you for helping me become free.'

Hopefully, you are able to see that the design stage is quite easy. The difficulty is knowing what the core limiting belief is, the one at the bottom of the well, to allow the empowering belief to be what you need to change. With the right empowering belief, the drop-down menu becomes easy in its design.

You might think the drop-down menus look pretty similar. 'Amanda,' you may say, 'surely all clients effectively have the same drop-down menus?' It is true, they are quite similar in design, but the wording means different things for different people. What seems generic on paper is powerful for the people who connect with this in their lives.

This is when the seemingly impossible becomes possible. They see, probably for the first time in their lives, that they have a choice. They have the power to change.

So do you.

7

You Can Delete What Doesn't Serve You

I have shared so much with you about how change is easier than many people think. My team and I help thousands of people from all walks of life delete what does not serve them quickly and easily. The best thing is it's pain free… well, almost.

What you have learned so far has taken you on a journey of self-discovery. You will know what is not serving you, what the limiting belief symptoms are that are showing up in your life. You probably won't know exactly what that limiting belief is yet; that's OK, you know the essence of it. You may even know what you want to move towards – your empowering belief – rather than just what you want to move away from. Again, this is self-discovery and design. It is powerful stuff.

What would life be like if you believed in you?

Let's go on an adventure and explore the empowerment side of the equation. Are you ready to play a game again?

I have the same request as in the last chapter. Please be alone, able to speak out loud and relax when you play this game. I can assure you that this will make it much more pleasurable for you. Read the questions – they're much the same as the ones in Chapter 6, but you'll be finding the answers through a different lens – and give yourself some time to answer each one before moving on.

If your conditions are perfect, then let's do this now. Alternatively, you can come back to this if you prefer.

Think about your empowering belief. Play along and say it out loud. Now think about how that empowering belief will transform the quality of your life. What will you gain by this new belief? Say this out loud.

How is your life greater? How is it more fulfilling, richer emotionally, physically and spiritually? What is your level of happiness? Answer these questions out loud.

What are you most grateful for because of having this empowering belief? Again, out loud.

Imagine that you have moved two years into the future and brought this new empowering belief with you. Everyone around you is two years older. The belief is two years older and has more power. Things have moved on; people have moved on.

How has this empowering belief affected your life? How has it affected your relationships, your emotional, physical and spiritual body, and your happiness? You know what to do – always answer aloud.

What are you most grateful for because of having this empowering belief?

Now move into your future by five years. Notice what has changed around you. How has this empowering belief affected your life, your relationships, your emotional, physical and spiritual body, and your level of happiness?

What are you most grateful for because of having this empowering belief?

Finally, move into your future by ten years and ask yourself the same questions. Speak the answers aloud.

As you did in the previous chapter, recognise that none of this has happened yet. You have the chance to change your life. Your unconscious mind has given you a glimpse of what your future could hold if you live out of your empowering belief. You have a choice. What would life be like if you really believed in you?

As your unconscious mind is designed to seek whole-ness, the exercise from this perspective would have been much more pleasurable than the first time you did it. Look at the person you can be in ten years' time and know that the journey there will also be much more pleasurable if you're running your empowering belief. This belief starts right away from installation and builds over time.

This is the great thing about changing your beliefs: the change lasts. I have been helping clients do this since 2005 and they report great changes as time goes by. One such client is a young woman in the UK who I worked with back in 2008. After attending a two-day workshop, she asked if she could do some one-on-one work with me, so we spent one hour together.

During the workshop, she'd uncovered that her limit-ing belief was that she was 'not good enough'. What she wanted to move towards was that she was capable of doing anything she put her mind to, so we did the belief-change process.

The client sent lots of fantastic feedback in the months following her belief change, and then got on with her own life. In 2021, completely out of the blue, she put a post on Facebook on our business page, thanking my team and me for the belief-change work we did thirteen years earlier.

Make sure the change is good for you

It is important to know that the people who receive this type of change are ready to change. They are not expecting a magic wand and know it will require them to come to the party.

There's another important factor too: the ecology must be aligned. Let me explain what ecology is.

As you now know, the unconscious mind is always seeking wholeness. As a result, it will resist anything that will cause harm to you or the people you care about. This includes the pain associated with the process of making a change.

Ecology is a way of checking that the change is right for you, ensuring that any change you make will serve you and those around you. You want to ensure that you only create change that does this. Without alignment in the ecology, change will not occur.

This may sound odd. Let me give you an example.

A DOUBTFUL YES

A client, Fiona, came to see me while I was in Portugal. She had moved to Portugal from the UK and, like many expats, had driven there as she had a fear of flying. She wanted to change this.

I could see how this was a problem for her. She had a son at university in the UK and was unable to visit him as she was so frightened of flying. The option of driving there and back every time was costly on both the pocket and time.

The change made logical sense, but my team and I always check alignment in the ecology with a simple question.

'Is it OK for your unconscious mind to make this change today and for you to be aware of this consciously?'

It's a simple yet unusual question. What it is really doing is asking the unconscious mind for permission to change, which is why it seems a little odd, but the client usually responds with a fully congruent yes, which means their whole being agrees. I asked the question of Fiona. She said yes automatically, which is what we look for when asking this question. No thought, just an automatic response. Then she faltered and said she was not sure.

Time to investigate. This is not a fully congruent yes.

AMANDA: What makes you unsure?

FIONA: I don't know, it just feels too big to make this change.

AMANDA: What about it feels too big?

FIONA: Well, as much as I want to see my son, there's another factor I hadn't considered until now.

AMANDA: That's good for you to know. What is it?

FIONA: I haven't seen my mum for years. We fell out; she was not a good mother. Now she is in a nursing home close to my son's university. If I get over my fear of flying, I am not sure if I will be able to go and see my son and deal with the guilt of not seeing her. I think it will be too much for me.

Sometimes the benefit that the client gets from having the problem outweighs the problem itself. It was almost as though Fiona's move to Portugal and her fear of flying had developed to give her an excuse not to see her mum.

We worked on her relationship with her mum in that session rather than the fear of flying. We looked at how her mum was doing the best she could with the resources she had at the time when she was raising Fiona and her sister. Fiona released her anger and other negative emotions that she had been carrying for such a long time about her mum and was able to forgive her, which meant we could move forward and work on what she had to come to see me for.

We worked on her fear of flying in our next session, once the issue with her mother had resolution and the ecology was aligned. Then we could, with the permission of her unconscious mind, do good work to solve that problem.

Sometimes a problem exists to create a get-out-of-jail card for the client. It means they have a 'reason' not to have to do things. Having the problem gives them 'benefits' that are at first not obvious, yet these benefits outweigh the problem itself.

Do you have benefits? What does having a problem give you that is positive? Be honest with yourself and think about how it has been your friend at times.

A limiting belief can give significant benefits to you. It can drive you to do better, be your motivation. It can be a constant daily reminder of what you are trying to move away from. The question, then, is how can you still have those benefits without having the problem?

As you have seen from Fiona's story, the so-called 'benefits' of a limiting belief are usually items on a drop-down menu, just like the symptoms of the limiting belief. In other words, there's something deeper down the well that the benefits are preventing you from confronting. As Fiona did, when you look at how changing your limiting belief to an empowering one will change your life, you're likely to uncover whatever it is that you're using the limiting belief as a 'reason' to avoid. Then you can work on that root issue, doing away with the need for the 'benefits' and reassuring your unconscious mind that no one will be hurt by the change.

As for positive things like drive and motivation, if you're running from an empowering rather than limiting belief, you will find these become natural to you. You won't need that limiting belief pushing and nagging at you all the time.

Having a problem like a limiting belief feels so permanent that change can seem impossible. In these cases, people often just prefer to keep it. How do I know that? Because when I work with them, some clients won't go there. Change is frightening, so they would prefer to work with what they perceive the problem to be, but this is only the drop-down menu: the symptoms of the limiting belief; the leaves of the weed.

You have seen the consequences for your life in ten years' time if you don't make a change. Let's look at what that change really means for you if your limiting beliefs feel permanent.

Your influence

Every time you communicate, you are influencing people around you, either positively or negatively. As the body image experiment that Dove conducted shows, your influence just happens. It is undeniable.

If you continue to live from the limiting belief, consider how its influence will spread out among those people you spend your time with. I don't just mean the little ones in your life; everyone you interact with on a day-to-day basis will be affected by how you're showing up. If you're showing up operating from a limiting belief, your influence is likely to be disempowering.

Most people think when they make a change, it only makes them feel better, enhances their life, but my team and I have noticed something that's equally important. Not only do they get the change they want, but the people around them are also affected much more positively because of who the person is now and how they are showing up. Their energy, positivity and vibrancy for life ripple out. Everybody wins.

On the other hand, if they continue to live without any change, the ripple effect will be echoing how they show up in the world.

One of life's biggest illusions is that you are what you are. People don't change; you are stuck with what you've been given. The truth is that we are all running limiting beliefs that hold us back. When we look at others' lives, we can tend to think how happy they seem; how successful, intelligent, healthy, fit, tall, whatever. There's a view that everyone else is doing just great and we are the only ones who are pretending.

It's an illusion. Having worked with thousands of people over the last twenty years, I have learned that even the most successful have their issues. When I say successful, I don't just mean financially; relationships, life choices, health, love and family are all measures of success and these people seem to have it all. Yet when I talk with them, when they are honest with themselves, they tell me how the success is just a distraction. It's like a shiny gold medal that has people looking at it, admiring it, but its appeal is short lived and empty.

Let's think about that for a moment.

GOING FOR GOLD

When an athlete is chasing an Olympic gold medal, what does this really mean for them? When I work with athletes who compete at this level, this is one of the questions I ask them.

'What will winning gold mean for you?'

I worked with an athlete who represented her country in the Winter Olympics. Margaux Hackett is a slopestyle skier and was preparing for her first time on this world stage. Her sport is risky and she had fallen a few times, resulting in bad concussion.

After the concussion, she had struggled with depression and suicidal thoughts and had some tough times. When we started to work together, we looked at what was underneath the success, what was driving her. She dug deep and changed her belief systems, became grounded. Now she knows who she is, sees her role as being one of influence and empowerment and has grown so much into who she was designed to be.

Recently, she put up a post on social media sharing her experience with mental health. Wanting to help others who may be feeling the same by telling her story, she was honest and raw. It was the ultimate in helping others by being vulnerable and exposing what is really going on under the illusion of perceived success.

What Margaux did was focus on herself rather than winning the gold. She gave herself the gift of who she really is. Even though she didn't get the result she wanted, she had a great Olympics; she thrived, she was herself and she loved it.

Long after the shine of a gold medal would have faded, Margaux's prize will last forever and grow every day. The prize she awarded herself was herself and the influence of others as she travels this life. Now that's what I call winning gold.

Sometimes, being connected with who you really are is the biggest gift you can give yourself. Really looking at what you believe about yourself and what might be holding you back can be refreshing, providing you know you can change. Hopefully, you do know this by now and see change as an opportunity.

WITHOUT CHANGE, THAT LIMITING BELIEF WILL FOLLOW YOU EVERYWHERE

One client, Jack, is senior in his family's business. He is doing a great job, he is happy at work. He has worked for his family for a long time and loves it. Yet, he wants to leave. He wants to make it on his own, feeling like life is too easy for him.

JACK: I need to make my own way. If I leave the family business, I can get a similar job on my own merit, not because I was born into this family.

AMANDA: OK, let me check that I understand. What you are saying is you're really enjoying your work and you're successful at it, but you would prefer to leave this job and go to another company to work in a similar role to feel that you're making it on your own. Is that right?

JACK: When you say it like that, it seems stupid.

AMANDA: I am just checking this is what you meant; I am not saying it in any way other than how you said it.

JACK: Yes, I see. It's stupid, but that's how I feel.

We went on a journey of discovery. Once we got to the bottom of his well, Jack realised that he was running a limiting belief that he is not worthy. Whenever he was running this limiting belief, he felt that he'd only made it because of the family business and not because of himself.

The interesting thing is that even if he left his family business and found a similar job in another company, while the limiting belief that he is not worthy was running, he would not feel worthy of any success he achieved. He couldn't escape, unless he made a change.

Which he did. Together, we changed his belief from the limiting 'I am not worthy' to the empowering 'I am worth all I attract and achieve in my life'. This meant Jack could see that it was his talent and skill that had got him to where he is in the company, not that he had been given the role because of who his family is. It was a big moment for Jack. His self-worth was reinstalled and he felt excited about what he would achieve going forward.

The world was at his feet. He did not need to jump ship to find that it was his limiting belief of worthlessness that was the issue and unless he changed this, it would always follow him. Changing company would never resolve the issue; it was in Jack and only he had the power to change it. Thankfully, he did.

You have heard a few client stories in this chapter. Have their experiences connected with you? Let's check in with you now. What are your thoughts? How is this sitting with you?

Shall we continue our journey and find out what is really going on at the bottom of the well? If your answer is yes – and if you've got this far, I hope it will be – what are the next steps?

8

You Can Reconnect With Your Inner Genius

Your unconscious mind is a genius. You are a genius.

In this chapter, let's take a closer look at what your unconscious mind really is. It is like getting to know a person well. First, you need to know how they tick, what they get up for every morning, what their hopes and dreams are. Understanding this will help you in your return to your genius.

Your unconscious mind is the part of you that is not conscious. Getting to know your unconscious mind, you need to look at what it does for you, how it helps you and... oh, this will likely blow your mind.

Your unconscious mind is the part of you that beats your heart around 10,000 times per day, regulates your blood pressure, wakes you up when your body has had a deep sleep. It is the core of your being. It has a blueprint for perfect health – you hurt yourself and the unconscious mind knows how to heal you.

The conscious mind is the thinking, logical brain. It can process between five to seven bits of information every second, which is not much when you compare it to the unconscious mind filtering 11,000,000 bits down to 148, right?

What your unconscious mind does for you

The unconscious mind has prime directives. These are things it is programmed to do for you. To keep you safe, it has around twenty prime directives, but here we will just focus on the eight main ones:

1. It stores all your memories. Not just memories of things that have happened, but memories of those that are yet to happen. We will come on to future memories in Chapter 10.

2. It stores and runs all your emotions. Every emotion you feel comes from your unconscious mind.

3. It organises all your memories according to time, knowing the difference between your past and future memories. This is why time is a good

healer. When you experience an event, you will only perceive the reality of it based on your filters at that time, but when you recall that memory, your filters will have changed so you will have a new perspective (or reality) on that event.

4. It represses harmful memories to keep you safe. In some cases of trauma, the sufferer will have no memory of the event that triggered it. When their system is more resourceful, when they are in a better place, then the memory can be reintroduced for resolution.

5. It has a blueprint for perfect health and is always seeking wholeness and wellness. In other words, it runs the body.

6. It is the powerhouse, the 'go getter', whereas the conscious mind is the 'goal setter'. You need to be mindful of your self-talk as your unconscious mind needs clear, precise directions to follow and whatever you say to yourself, it will be listening to, judgment free, and acting on.

Recently, I was concerned about driving my VW campervan in Portugal. I did not have a copy of my driving licence with me – I had lost it on the way from New Zealand to Portugal – so I was worried about being pulled over by the police and fined for not having it in my possession.

I printed out all my documents, had digital copies on my phone and prepared a file in case I got pulled over. The next day, I was involved in a small bump and the other driver called the police, as is the law in Portugal. I could not believe it!

Then I realised that I had been thinking about getting pulled over to the point where I had got everything 'ready'. All the paperwork I needed was in the campervan, so I had literally told my unconscious mind what I wanted and it was delivered. I should have focused on what I really wanted instead of what I did not want.

7. It stores all your learnings. Once you have learned a skill, it is then passed to your unconscious mind so it's there for you whenever you need it.

   Think about when you learned to drive a car. At the time, it felt quite overwhelming because this learning needed your conscious mind, but once you'd mastered the skill, then the driving of a car passed to the unconscious mind. The last time you drove, you were probably thinking about something completely different because your unconscious mind was the part of you controlling the car.

8. It stores all your habits to run automatically without you even thinking about it. Some habits you have will be really good for you and some you'll wish you didn't have. If you want to change a habit, then you must change it at an unconscious level. Willpower just won't cut it.

The genius that is the unconscious mind is doing so much more for you than perhaps you realise. We all tend to live in such a conscious world where the unconscious mind is given little time and energy. Hopefully, by understanding some of the things it does for you automatically and underneath the radar, you'll now have a greater appreciation for the genius you have inside of you.

How do you reconnect with your inner genius?

Think about the last time you had a gut feeling. Perhaps logically, it made sense to make one decision, but you really felt that was the wrong thing to do. On paper, it may have seemed that the gut decision would never work. I suspect the outcome if you went with the gut feeling would have been far more favourable than if you'd followed what seemed the better, more logical option.

Interestingly, the gut feeling is coming from your unconscious mind. This is the part of you that is the genius and, in many respects, all knowing. Do you listen to that part of you, or do you go with a conscious, logical decision?

I have learned over the years that my unconscious mind always knows what is best for me, if only I listen. I was in New Zealand when I got a phone call from my sister saying that my dad had been taken into hospital. It wasn't life-threatening; he had a chest infection. I even spoke to the medical team who told me that Dad was stable and there was no need to come over, other than to see the family. Nonetheless, my sister wondered if I might be able to come back to the United Kingdom from New Zealand a little bit earlier than I'd planned to help take Mum to the hospital to visit him every day.

I was due to speak at a major event in Brisbane, Australia, where I was doing a keynote. I had planned to fly to Brisbane to deliver the talk, and then fly on from there to London. The plans were all made and I was due to leave in a few days' time.

I went for a run around my local lake. It was a run that I did regularly as I love being out in nature. While running, I had the overwhelming feeling that I needed to leave immediately. I needed to cancel the talk in Brisbane and get myself to London as quickly as possible.

I came home and shared this with Sarah. It seemed completely the wrong thing to do. It was not the logical thing to do. The medical staff had told me that Dad was OK, so I was only heading back to help my family.

I acted on my gut feeling and thank goodness I did. When I arrived at London Gatwick, I went straight to the hospital. My beautiful dad passed away twenty-two hours later. If I'd have gone with the original plans, I would most certainly have missed our precious goodbye.

This is the power of the unconscious mind. It is all knowing; it is like it has a direct line to the Universe. If you listen, then you will be amazed at what it can do for you.

Take a moment to think about when your unconscious mind has wanted to communicate something with you. More importantly, be curious about when it will show up next. You might even want to have a conversation with your unconscious mind to thank it for everything it has done and everything it continues to do for you. Let it know that you're open to being curious about the next time it wants to communicate something directly with you.

It may feel a little odd having this type of conversation with yourself, but what have you got to lose? There is only everything to gain. Your unconscious mind will continue running your entire system with or without you, but if you embark on developing a relationship with it, this in itself is powerful.

What I find interesting is this: when we were born, we came with everything we needed for life already installed. All the apps were running. We were whole. We were perfect.

Then as we get older, life causes a few of the apps to get glitchy. We become fragmented and lose the ability to connect with the inner genius that's inside us all. It's like we forget who we are, and that's when we lose our way.

Let's find our way back to wholeness

This will take curiosity and trust.

When students come to our courses, my team and I always talk about the subject of developing a relationship with the unconscious mind. The way we do this is through a guided hypnosis every morning and evening on a live course and we encourage online students to listen to the hypnosis as much as they can.

You might have your own ways of meditating or a relaxation technique that you really enjoy, so feel free to use this, but if you would like to access the ones I have created for our students, you will find the links in the Further Resources section at the end of the book. During the course, students really deepen their relationship with their unconscious mind. They start to have signals, feelings, insights and an intuition that is finely tuned. This all points to the fact that they are now, for the first time, developing a relationship with a part of them that is the genius. All this over a seven-day course.

For most people, realising that they have something as powerful as the unconscious mind is a little bit magical. Back in 2005 when I first learned about it, I was almost disbelieving of the fact that it even existed, and yet I was extremely grateful to be given the knowledge and, better still, the ability to develop a deeper relationship with this part of me.

As we learned earlier, the unconscious mind stores all our values and beliefs. We also know that these are installed at a young age, before we're seven, and are formed by other people through influence. What's important about developing a relationship with our unconscious mind is this gives us the ability to communicate with the part of us where if changes are made, they become unimaginable.

Another way to connect with your unconscious mind is to have gratitude around what it does for you. Now you have a better understanding of what your unconscious mind is doing for you on a daily basis, minute by minute, there's lots to be grateful for.

Gratefulness has a place in everybody's life, so spending a little time each day thanking your unconscious mind for all it does for all of you will deepen your appreciation and your relationship with this inner-genius part of you. It may be as simple as each morning thanking your unconscious mind for waking you up, for beating your heart, for allowing you to learn as easily as you have all the things you have learned and will learn.

What will you start with? Think of a few things and start tonight before you drift off to sleep. Thank your inner genius like you would thank an old friend who has done something you are truly grateful for. Then notice whatever you notice. It might be your intuition showing up more; it might be you feel more connected, grounded, at ease or at peace.

Expect to see, feel or hear new things. If your intention is that your unconscious mind will show itself more to you, then it will; if you think this is a load of old rubbish and nothing will change, it won't. Your unconscious mind will show up, it always has. What changes is whether you are listening.

Mentalist and illusionist Derren Brown, based in the UK, has been appearing on Channel 4, a British TV channel, for years. In fact, he has become a little bit of a national treasure.

What Derren does is referred to as psychological magic, but what he's really doing is using a combination of NLP and hypnosis to allow people to do things that seem quite magical. In other words, he is programming his subjects.

He created a programme on British TV called *Intervention* in which he met a young woman, Emily, in a café to tell her that she'd been selected to be on his Channel 4 show. Over the next two weeks, he told her, actors would be showing up in her life, and even her family and friends may be asked by the producers to act in a certain way. Their interventions were all designed to create positivity and a realisation that she was so much more than she thought she was. The link to the programme is in the 'Further Resources' section if you wish to watch it.

To show Emily how easy it was to create an intervention in her life, he told her that the gentleman sitting around 100 metres away from them was about to spill her water. A sequence of events then led to him indeed spilling her water, which impressed Emily so much, she fully believed that over the next two weeks, actors, friends and family would be intervening in her life in a certain way because they had been asked to by the TV show producer.

Derren asked Emily to create video diaries every day for the next two weeks. Before she heard about the programme, she'd had low self-esteem and a lack of confidence in her abilities. She really felt she didn't have much to offer.

Through her video diaries, the viewer saw how she was starting to recognise opportunities that she had not experienced before. Her confidence was building and she now felt that she had lots to offer people. She thought she had changed as a result of all the interventions that had been put into place by Derren Brown's programme.

In actual fact, her family and friends did nothing different.

Nothing at all.

There were no actors.

There were no interventions.

Every opportunity presented itself because she was looking through different filters. The environment was the same; the 11 million bits of information bombarding her neurology were unchanged; but her filters were looking for a different 148 bits. They were looking for positivity, self-esteem, worthiness, and that's what she found.

The only things that had changed were her filters; her intentions; her expectations. Life was happening for her.

When she appeared on the show two weeks later, Derren Brown shared with Emily that Channel 4 had changed nothing about her environment. She couldn't believe it. He told her that the change in her was all her doing. It was all to do with the way she was choosing to look at life now that allowed her to see things that she could never see before.

She was blown away.

LOOK FOR YOUR MAGIC

Suzy is a client I worked with in Portugal. After our first session together, she did the same exercise I am asking you to do: she recognised everything that her unconscious mind does for her, how it is all knowing and will always suggest what is best for her, even if it doesn't seem to make logical sense. She then learned to be grateful to her inner genius and assure it that she will always listen to it.

AMANDA: How did you find the exercise I gave you last week?

SUZY: I love the gratefulness exercise. It's something that I have tried to practise in the past, but I found it a little bit false, like I was just pretending to be grateful. When you talked me through how to have gratefulness for the unconscious part of me operating my perfect blueprint for health and waking me up every day, it then came easily.

The other thing I really love about the exercise is that I've started to notice things that I hadn't noticed before, even in my close relationships such as with my children and my husband. I think my filters must've been deleting kind words they have said to me. Perhaps I have not been looking at their faces in the past to see that they really meant what they said.

AMANDA: That's great to hear. All you've done is develop a deeper relationship with your unconscious mind and it's already showing you how to look differently at your life.

Suzi: I've also noticed that I seem to be enjoying work more. I'm starting to see that actually, I'm an important part of the team and I've got some great friendships there. Interestingly, my reasons for wanting to stay clear of some people were all just in my head. I hadn't really seen those people for what they really were – caring people – before I did this exercise. Yes, I have enjoyed it and I am excited to see what is next.

Be the star of your own show. Look for the magic. Look at everything like life is happening for you and notice what you notice.

9
You Can Uncover Your Deepest Unknowns

Earlier on in the book, we learned that if you can name your limiting belief, then that's not it. The simple reason for this is that if you can name the limiting belief, it is running in the conscious mind, and as we all know now, you are looking for a core limiting belief that's running underneath the radar. The one that's at the bottom of the well runs unconsciously, which means you are not able to name it.

All you would be doing if you worked with the limiting belief that you can name is pruning the weed by taking off a few leaves. What you're interested in is being able to get the weed by the root and pull it up for good, never to grow back.

What it is important to notice is that the deepest unknowns are housed in the unconscious mind. To be able to uncover them, you need to work with the unconscious mind. Let's try it out.

Name your limiting belief out loud. If you are surrounded by people, then just say it inside to yourself. I have asked you to think about this several times throughout the book and the reason I've done this is to bring you to this place here, right now. The fact that you've considered it before probably means you can name your limiting belief now.

That's not it.

Even though you have thought about it, it is still coming from your conscious mind. It is just a symptom and not at the bottom of the well. Your core limiting belief remains unknown.

PULLING THE WEED UP BY THE ROOTS

Here's how this looked for a client, Jude.

AMANDA: If you were to have a guess at what your limiting belief is, what would you say?

JUDE: That I am not good enough, I think.

I noticed that there was no emotion attached to this statement when Jude said it. I know when we're getting further down the well and into the realms of the unconscious because there's always emotion when the client speaks of the limiting belief. It feels true to them. There's pain.

AMANDA: Does that feel real to you?

JUDE: Yes, it feels real. Sometimes, I don't feel I am good enough. For example, the other day, I was with a good friend of mine. We meet quite often to have lunch and she told me that she thought the outfit I was wearing was really lovely. I smiled and thanked her, and then immediately followed it up with the fact that I'd got it cheap in the sale and I'd had it for many years. I guess it's because I don't feel I'm good enough to be able to go out and buy new clothes at full price.

AMANDA: Great observation, Jude, you've got self-awareness, but the fact you can name the limiting belief means that's not it. It might be close, yet there is something deeper down the well. Once we have found what it is, deleted it and installed a new empowering belief, it will make a huge difference for you.

Jude and I continued to work together. Over the next few sessions, she had a huge breakthrough: we uncovered her core limiting belief, deleted it, created her new empowering beliefs and installed them.

Jude felt so much relief just knowing what the limiting belief was. She also knew that for sixty-five years, she had been living from a place of feeling worthless and dirty. She was five years old when this belief was installed in her, so this was not her fault. For the first time in her life, she felt free; she felt light; she felt like herself.

If we had worked with 'I am not good enough', it would still have helped Jude. It would just not have given her the breakthrough she deserved.

What happens if we don't go to the bottom of the well? If we merely trim the leaves of the weed rather than pulling it up by the roots?

THE RIPPLE EFFECTS OF TRIMMING THE LEAVES

I worked with a seventeen-year-old client called Beatrice. She was the head girl at a local school who had an invitation to do something called Outward Bound. This involved her joining other people of her age on outdoor adventures such as hiking, swimming, kayaking and building survival shelters.

That was all fine. Then Beatrice found out that at the end of the two-week Outward Bound experience, she would need to run a half marathon. This was terrible for Beatrice because she was a self-proclaimed couch potato. Even taking the bins out on a Sunday evening was too much for Beatrice; she just loathed exercise.

She had done some work with me previously and knew the power of her neurology, if the reprogramming was done well, so she called to see if she could have a belief-change session with me. When I asked Beatrice in the session what it was she wanted to change, she said this:

'I believe that I am not a fit and healthy person, and I would rather believe that I am fit and healthy.'

Beatrice could clearly name the belief that she knew would limit her while she was on her Outward Bound experience, but this was at the top of the well. However, it was important that I worked with this as a limiting belief because it was the belief system that was causing Beatrice all her current problems.

We did the belief change in that session, then Beatrice went home to her mum, Vicki. Vicki was training to do an event called the Routeburn. This is generally a four-day hike in New Zealand, but Vicki was training to do it in one day. This was going to be a big challenge for Vicki, even though she was very fit.

I can imagine Vicki's dismay when Beatrice came home after the belief change and announced that she would like to join her on the challenge. I got a phone call from Vicki immediately, asking what I had done to her daughter. There was no way that Beatrice could possibly join her two days later to do the challenge because she hadn't done any training.

I suggested to Vicki that if Beatrice believed she could do it to support her. Vicki took my advice and Beatrice finished the challenge, actually pretty easily. She even filmed a video for me at the top of the highest climb and it's now on my website. Beatrice is more than happy to share the difference that this has made to her life.

That was five years ago and Beatrice now lives in New York, practises yoga and runs daily. She calls herself an exerciser and really doesn't like it if she's not able to exercise regularly. She has given herself one of the biggest gifts a young person can give themselves and that is to keep herself fit and healthy. Even though the belief system we worked on that day was at the top of the well for Beatrice, the ripple effect it has had throughout her life is incredible.

I'm not saying that you need to go to the bottom of the well every time you work on a limiting belief. Perhaps the one that you can name will give you the same kind of ripple effect that Beatrice experienced. There's no judgment, but the lower you go, the more powerful the belief change is.

How do you get to the bottom of the well?

TRAVELLING DOWN THE WELL, ONE BELIEF AT A TIME

When a client, Paul, came to me, I asked him some stealth-like questions that would take us down to the bottom of his well. The idea was that we'd start with a symptom, then look at what was underneath it.

AMANDA: What do you think the limiting belief is, Paul? If you were to guess, what would it be?

PAUL: That I am stupid, that I don't know as much as others. I have always felt this way.

AMANDA: OK, thanks for that. This is a good place to start. Let me ask you what it is you believe about yourself that causes you to think that you're stupid.

PAUL: Oh now, that's a tough question. Probably that I'm just not intelligent.

AMANDA: If you believe you are not intelligent, what is it you believe about yourself that causes you to think that?

Long pause with no eye contact. Paul uncrosses his legs and looks at his feet.

PAUL: That I'm broken, like there's something wrong with me.

AMANDA: Good, you're doing really well, Paul. What do you believe about yourself that causes you to think that you're broken?

Paul is now shifting around on the sofa. He's twiddling his fingers, his expression trancelike, almost as though he's daydreaming.

A long pause. A big sigh.

PAUL: (whispering) I'm a mistake.

His eyes well up, his voice is restricted. He looks down and breathes a huge sigh. Of relief.

He looks up at me.

PAUL: That's it, I'm a mistake. It makes perfect sense; it all makes sense.

AMANDA: How does this make sense to you?

PAUL: I'm adopted; I was a mistake. I was never wanted.

AMANDA: Even by your adoptive parents?

PAUL: No, they loved me and wanted me. I had a fabulous childhood and they sacrificed a lot for me, I know that. I mean that I have always felt that I was a mistake, not wanted, a nuisance. I think that is because right from the beginning, when my birth mother found out she didn't want me, at some level, I knew that, deep down where it is hidden away.

What Paul is describing here is a classic example of a limiting belief that has been installed in the womb. His deepest level believed that he was a mistake.

Let's think about this for a moment: all the conversations that his birth mother would have had while she was carrying him; all the plans that she would have made to prepare for his adoption. Then there was the birth and the care Paul needed prior to being adopted. Finally, he was placed with a family who loved and cared for him.

It's not a case of whether his birth mum wanted him or not. The conversations and the energy surrounding placing a child for adoption, her protection mechanism for her to be able to go ahead and give her child away, meant his unconscious mind learned even before birth that he was a mistake, that he was not wanted. As I mentioned earlier, the unconscious mind has no judgment. It follows the suggestions made by the conscious mind, and then goes out into the Universe to find evidence to support them and installs the limiting belief. In Paul's case, this was 'I am a mistake'.

We worked with this limiting belief, then worked on what he would rather believe about himself. This took time and required him to do some work alone at home using the Sherlock Holmes Process, which we will come to later in this chapter. He finally landed on 'I am loved and important'.

We deleted the limiting belief and installed the new one. For Paul, it was like night had turned to day. He felt the change immediately; the evidence of the belief change was tangible for him. His wife said he was so much happier and at ease with who he was, less anxious and sleeping better.

For Paul, this was the missing piece. He had done lots of work on himself before, but mainly on the symptoms and not the real issue. To him, it made so much sense. It showed why his life had been the way it had been and what was now possible for him.

How to get to the bottom of your well

In Paul's case, it was easy. A few well-timed and pertinent questions took him down to the core limiting belief, but it is not always that simple. The limiting belief may be so well hidden in the unconscious mind, we have to be a little creative.

Around fourteen years ago, I created something called the Sherlock Holmes Process. It came about when I was working with a client who was struggling to get to the bottom of the well. My unconscious mind came up with the idea, so I tested it with her and it worked. I ran it again and again with other clients and got the same results: each time, we got to the bottom of the well and uncovered their deepest unknowns.

What is great about this process is that it removes you from the focus, allowing you to imagine another person and access information about this person. In other words, you see yourself from a different perspective.

What did I do that first day? I asked my client to imagine that from our window, out in the garden we could see a woman standing on the lawn. She had her back to us and her arms folded, her head looking at the ground. Even though we couldn't see her facial expression, we knew that she was deep in thought and not feeling so good.

As we observed this lady out in the garden, we captured her thoughts. We could see them rising in a thought bubble from her lowered head.

I then repeated some of the symptoms the client had shared with me:

- I can't take a compliment.
- I don't think I'm good enough.
- Sometimes, I don't think I have anything of value to say.
- Sometimes, I think people think I'm a bit silly.

Whatever the client had shared with me as being the symptoms operating from their limiting belief, I spoke out loud, making sure I used exactly the client's words and not my own wording. I didn't interpret what each symptom might mean for me; it needed to be exactly as the client had said it.

I then let this sit with the client. For each thing we observed the lady out in the garden thinking, I gently asked this question of the client.

'If you were to have a guess, what do you think that lady really believes about herself that has caused her to have that thought?'

There was a long silence as the client pondered this, then she responded with something that was real genius. She added all the symptoms together and came up with whatever was at the bottom of the well for the lady on the lawn.

You've probably guessed it: the person out on the lawn was my client.

I asked the client to say this to herself and watched her reaction.

It created emotion; she had uncovered her deepest unknown and it felt so real and painful, but it also felt like the truth and made sense to her.

This process works well every time, whether the client is working online or in person. My team and I can pretty much guarantee that we will be able to get to what is really going on for the client using the Sherlock Holmes Process.

I'm now going to encourage you to do an exercise, a way of observing yourself in the Sherlock Holmes Process mode. If you really want to uncover your deepest unknowns, then this simple exercise, which you will do over the next forty-eight hours, will allow you to learn so much more about what's really going on for you.

It's your turn to be your own Sherlock Holmes

The Sherlock Holmes Process is great to run once you understand about limiting beliefs and how they operate in your neurology. This is exactly where you are right now. You know how damaging they can be.

To run this process well, select a time that is your 'normal' life. You could be working or at home, but make sure whatever you're doing is in your normal routine. Avoid a time where you're away on holiday or doing anything that is out of the ordinary. When you are ready and the time is right, run this process.

Over the next forty-eight hours, catch yourself every time you have a negative thought. Stop and, where possible, move yourself from the space that you had the negative thought in. For example, if you are sitting at your desk when you have the thought, stand up and move away from that space. Perhaps stand to the side of your desk.

Now get your Sherlock Holmes on.

You are not you; now, you are your own Sherlock Holmes and you are going to ask this about the person who was sitting at your desk:

'What is it that (insert your name) believes about themselves that caused them to think that?'

If I were running this process as the one wanting to find out my deepest unknown, I would have the negative thought, stand up, move to the side and say, 'What is it that Amanda believes about herself that caused her to think that?' Then I would wait.

There will be some great feedback. Our brains are designed to answer questions and the quality of the answer will be determined by the quality of the question.

IF WE ASK A POOR QUESTION, WE GET A POOR ANSWER

Here's what happened with a client called Lottie when I explained the Sherlock Holmes Process to her.

AMANDA: You're going to be your own Sherlock Holmes. This means you'll eavesdrop on your internal dialogue, which you're already good at doing because you've put it down on this piece of paper. (Amanda holds up the paper Lottie had filled in earlier. These are the client notes that a client sends prior to a session.) You're even able to tell me that happens about four times a week and your internal dialogue generally revolves around you being lazy or not doing enough.

Forget the context of this. What I want you to do is observe any time you have a negative thought.

135

Step away from the space you were in when you had that thought. The question I then want you to ask yourself is, 'What is it that Lottie believes about herself that caused her to think that?' I'll let you write that down, and then I'll continue.

LOTTIE: Great, OK, I have that written down now.

AMANDA: Yeah, the structure of the question is important. You ask yourself 'What is it that Lottie believes about herself that caused her to think that?' not 'What is it I believe about myself?'

LOTTIE: That's actually what I wrote.

AMANDA: You become Sherlock Holmes. We want to be quite playful; it doesn't want to be like, 'Oh God, there we go.' You don't want to get too emotionally pent up about it.

Be quite playful, a bit pantomiming.

LOTTIE: OK.

AMANDA: Just see what comes up for you. The quality of the question that we ask determines the quality of the information we gain, so avoid asking why. It's a really poor-quality question and it spirals.

LOTTIE: Yeah, like, 'Why do I think that? Why do I always do that?'

AMANDA: Yes that's right. 'Why' spirals down and doesn't give any really good information. Asking what it is Lottie believes about herself that causes her to think a certain thing will allow you to access far better information. It also does another really cool thing: it causes you to interrupt the pattern.

A pattern interrupt is where you are now conscious of the program that runs unconsciously. Just being aware of it gives you great power and here's why: you are able to interrupt that pattern. This means the pattern can no longer run underneath the radar. It's almost like you have outed it, caught it red-handed.

Now you are able to say, 'No, sorry, I'm not running your program. I am inspecting it, so stop right there.'

The program that would normally run from a negative thought to a behaviour – as thoughts become things – is now halted. It will not be able to run its usual path, which tends to be a sabotaging behaviour such as over-eating, punishing yourself with a cycle of negative narratives, running an unhelpful internal movie, saying no to things you know you would enjoy – in essence, railroading your happiness. The pattern interrupt means that you will get a better outcome while you run this program, but it is not permanent. It is only effective while you are your own Sherlock Holmes. This is how you uncover the deepest unknowns, using the process of observation and listening to what your unconscious mind reveals to you.

You will notice in Lottie's narrative that we talked about being playful. The more playful you can be, the better. Be light about this process. The subject is important, but being heavy and serious about it will not deliver the best results; it will only push away the information and leave you with a self-analytical mindset, so be playful and curious.

Whatever comes up for you, have gratitude around it. Thank your unconscious mind for what it has given you. Once the information comes, let it be what it is. No analysis, just gratitude that you are on a journey of self-discovery.

When I am guiding a client to uncover the unknown, I am looking for the gap between the gap. That's the pause between the narrative, which is where the unconscious mind feels what is real rather than in the language the client uses. The unconscious mind works at the speed of light. It 'gets it', so notice what happens – the feelings, the sensations in your body – as you do the Sherlock Holmes Process.

Start your Sherlock Holmes forty-eight hours today. Gather your information and I can assure you that you will be guided to what your deepest unknown is, your limiting belief.

Once you have this information, you will need to know what to do next.

How to delete your limiting belief and install your new one

Now you know your deepest unknowns, what do you do with that information?

If you are a coach and reading this book for your personal development, then I am delighted and thank you for trusting me to be your guide. If you are reading this for you, to change your life, then know that you have already uncovered so much vital information. You will feel your self-awareness and understanding of what is going on for you in your life. You know what your limiting belief is, or at least the essence of it, and perhaps what your new empowering belief is, along with the drop-down menu for each. You know what needs deleting and installing; you are on your way to being the architect of your life.

How do you do the process of deleting and installing? When your phone or computer goes wrong, what do you do? You take it to an expert who is highly trained in understanding which programs might be glitchy. They know what to do, and quickly, to give you the outcome that you want.

A belief change is the same. You need to connect with someone who knows what they are doing, is trained and has experience with the belief-change process.

Your time spent with me has been worthwhile. You now only need to run the belief-change process as opposed to spending time uncovering the unknown. Knowing what you know now, you have a different way of thinking, which makes it so much easier for the expert facilitating the belief change. In many respects, you have done the hard work in uncovering or getting close to your limiting belief. The rest takes about one hour, and then you will have your old limiting belief deleted and your new empowering belief installed.

If you are a coach, then please ensure you are trained, accredited and approved to run the Submodality Belief Change Process. If you want to become trained, then head to the 'Further Resources' section and I will point you in the right direction.

If you're working on yourself, please take action. The coach you choose to work with needs to be trained in the Submodality Belief Change Process, so ask about their experience with this process. How many belief changes have they done? Also ask for testimonials. What are their results?

Make sure you are in good hands. Then go for it.

10
What's Next?

By now, you will hopefully have run your Sherlock Holmes Process. What came up for you? What is your limiting belief? What would you rather believe instead?

Now you are all set to take action on what you uncovered from Sherlock Holmes. If you haven't done so yet, then head to the 'Further Resources' section where I have a link to connect you with people who can help.

This last chapter will make more sense if you have deleted your limiting belief and installed your new empowering one. That way, you are seeing your world through the filters of your new belief and not your limiting belief. If the timing is not right, though, that's fine. Read on anyway. If you have experienced anxiety, then this chapter will be a big help to you.

You can create and design your future

The truth here is that we are constantly creating an idea of our future; we just don't know that because it is out of conscious awareness. Think about this for a moment. Think of an event that is happening soon, maybe something that you're really looking forward to.

The chances are, perhaps without you realising it, you have already created a movie, probably with a soundtrack, of that event. You've gone out into your future and created a representation of what the event will be for you.

The reason that I suggest you think about an event you're looking forward to is this: to get excited about that event, you must have created a movie with a soundtrack. It will probably have some self-talk in there, too; maybe you could even taste or smell something related to it.

If I'd asked you to think about an event in the future that worries you, something that you're fearful of, then the same thing would happen in the neurology. You would create a movie with the components listed above, but when this movie runs with all these components, it would cause anxiety in your system. If the movie is an event you are looking forward to, then this creates excitement in the system.

The neurology runs the same way whether it's a positive or a negative movie, just as it does with an empowering or limiting belief. It has no judgment; it just operates in the same fashion, but gives us a different outcome.

People who experience anxiety a lot in their lives are good at doing this. Their internal movie is an unconscious program that runs out of conscious awareness, so they are unaware of what is happening. When I work with a client who runs anxiety as a daily program, often the realisation that this is something they're creating within their own neurology is a huge sigh of relief for them. What this means is that they can now do something different that will give them a different outcome.

ACTIVE IMAGINATION

When I'm running my live courses or speaking at a keynote, I generally reference a gentleman called Lewis Pugh. Lewis is an incredible guy: he decided that he would swim 1 km at the North Pole to build awareness around the fact that the ice caps are melting. To put this into perspective, the people who fell off the *Titanic* landed into water at 5°C. Water freezes at 0°C and the water at the North Pole is -1.7°.

It's really cold.

Lewis was unable to train his body in this temperature of water because nowhere is colder than the North Pole, so in his TED talk, he speaks about how he trained his mind to train his body to survive this 1 km swim. His coach and medical team felt that this was a huge risk. As he was unable to train his body physically for this temperature of water, he risked having a cardiac arrest because of the cold.

What Lewis did was create a movie that he ran in his mind hundreds of times while he was in the comfort of his apartment in London, sitting on his sofa. He used what's called active imagination to create this movie.

Unlike passive imagination, which only uses one sense: sight, active imagination incorporates all the senses:

- Visual / sight

- Auditory / sound (external)

- Kinaesthetic / feelings (external, not emotional)

- Olfactory / smell

- Gustatory / taste

- Internal dialogue / self-talk

Our senses allow us to experience the world. Without them, we are lost. We use the same senses to create the movie, just as Lewis did.

The interesting thing is that the unconscious mind does not know the difference between what is real and what is imagined. It treats them both exactly the same.

Just read that again.

This is very powerful.

Thoughts become things

Dr Deepak Chopra wrote a book called *Quantum Healing*. In it, he talks about neurotransmitters, which eavesdrop on our thoughts and connect the mind and body as one. We literally are what we think, and, in 1989, Deepak Chopra proved that what we think affects what we do, how we feel and our outcomes.

This is what was happening for Lewis. As he was sitting on the sofa running his movie, his body temperature would rise by 3°. His medical team found this incredible. He was sitting in his apartment in an ambient temperature and his body was behaving as though it was in freezing cold water. This is a perfect example of the neurotransmitters eavesdropping on the movie that he created, allowing his body to think that this is real and proving that the mind does not know the difference between what is imagined and what is actually happening in real time.

Sarah, my wife, played cricket for England for twelve years. She played in test matches, competed for the

Ashes and played all over the world. In fact, she was the first woman to play county cricket with the men; she turned up to Headingly cricket ground as the captain and the opposing team thought she was the scoreboard lady.

She was at the top of her game and became an all-rounder in the sport. Unfortunately, she broke her back playing cricket, which ended her career prematurely. When she learned about active imagination and neurotransmitters, a huge penny dropped for her. She could not believe that during all her years of playing cricket at such a high level, the sport psychologist she worked with had only been using passive imagination. In fact, most athletes only ever use passive imagination.

When my team and I introduce the concept of active imagination to athletes and Olympians, they totally get it. It makes perfect sense to them. Not only that, but the results they achieve are far greater than they would gain from passive imagination. Active imagination was directly responsible for Lewis being able to swim 1 km in water at -1.7° and swim it successfully.

The same thing happens when you run anxiety in your system. You project your mind out into the future and see/hear/feel an event going wrong. The mind doesn't know the difference between what is real and what is imagined, so flight or fight kicks in and you feel anxiety in your system, real time.

ANXIETY IS AN EMOTION OF THE FUTURE

I was emailed by a client called John who shared with me that he was about to embark on his own personal Everest. He had decided that he wanted to learn to swim. Not only that, but he was going to swim an ocean challenge called the Swim Noosa.

What was particularly impressive about John was that he was going to do this event on his seventieth birthday. He had trained his body; he was fit and perfectly capable of swimming the distance. Then he had gone with his friends to the ocean to swim the Noosa challenge distance.

The sea was rough that day. As all of them headed into the water, a huge wave went straight over John's head. It happened so quickly that he swallowed water and couldn't breathe properly.

Being submerged in the water, unable to breathe, was obviously scary for him. When he surfaced, his friends were already navigating their way through the breakers to the quieter water where they started to swim. For the first time in all his swimming training, John felt anxious. That short episode under the water had been enough to create a powerful internal movie that did not end well.

The unconscious mind's prime directive is to keep us alive, so John's flight or fight had kicked in. He made his way back to the beach and sat on the sand, waiting for his friends to complete their training swim. The thought of going back into the water was frightening for him. This movie had power and it felt real, and it had caused a problem for John. The challenge was on Saturday and this was Wednesday.

147

I booked a session with him on the Thursday afternoon, telling him that we would only need one session that would last sixty minutes. John was concerned as we didn't have long and his perception was that change takes time. He felt that he was running of time before the event.

He was also curious to see what he could do to help himself, so he came with an open mind, wanting to overcome this new situation: whenever he thought about entering the water, he created the state of anxiety.

I explained to John that he was creating this himself without realising. John totally got it and breathed a sigh of relief.

JOHN: If I am creating this myself, this means I can uncreate it, right?

AMANDA: You've got it, yes, and as quickly as you created the anxiety in the first place.

JOHN: That's such a relief; I thought we might need more time. It's so important to me to do this swim, it is my own personal Everest. Swimming has never been my strong point, so to do this would mean the world to me.

AMANDA: The good news is that you are skilled at creating the anxiety, so you are already using your active imagination. What we are going to use is exactly the same strategy, but change some things which will make a huge difference for you.

The reason I am sharing this with you now is because it is important to notice that whether you are running anxiety or excitement, the same thing is happening inside your neurology. A fully sensory movie is running under the radar. You have no conscious awareness apart from the sensation in your body, which is taking you either closer to or further away from the outcome you want. In John's case, it was further away.

He had a choice, as do you. You can choose to design your future.

How to design your future

My team and I run a live and online course called Seize Your Life. It was developed back in 2009 and does what it says on the can: it helps you to take control. The ultimate carpe diem.

Thousands of students have achieved their goals thanks to seizing their lives. They have:

- Lost 19 kg and kept it off for fifteen years since doing the course

- Found a life partner and had a family

- Emigrated and started a new life

- Left an abusive relationship to be safe

- Lived a clean drug-free life

- Written a book

- Started a successful business

- Bought a 7 Series BMW

- Run a marathon

- Been selected for the Olympics

- Represented their country and won a boxing match as the underdog

- Reduced cancerous tumours in the body

I used to call them goals, but it never felt right. It felt too 1980s and corporate. Then one day the penny dropped.

All these students had one thing in common: they'd created a future memory. I have been teaching this course for over thirteen years, taking the students through the powerful process of creating a compelling movie using all the senses.

Our unconscious mind stores all our memories in something called the hippocampus and uses something called the reticular activating system (RAS) to retrieve them. It goes a little like this.

Imagine you're out for dinner with a group of friends and one shares that they've really enjoyed watching a movie called *Inception*.

'It's got the actor in it,' they say. 'You know the one. Oh my goodness, I can't remember his name. He was in *Titanic* and *Wolf on Wall Street*. What's his name?'

Soon, everyone around the table is going, 'Yeah, I can see him, but I can't remember his name. It's on the tip of my tongue.'

Your RAS spirals into activity. It goes through all your memories, doing a match on the visual that you've got on the actor, collating the information. It is literally going through your filing cabinet of memories to retrieve the information you need to be able to name him.

Then at eleven o'clock at night, just as you're brushing your teeth, the name Leonardo DiCaprio springs to mind. Your RAS has done its job. It has used your memories to match and give you the answer.

We have past memories and future memories. When we use our active imagination to create a movie, we are creating a future memory. The unconscious mind is then expecting that memory to show up in our future and once again, it doesn't differentiate between a positive or negative memory.

People who create future memories tend to live them. They are doers rather than dreamers, but most people only dream.

The difference between dreamers and doers

Dreamers only have a faded hope to look back on when they get to their twilight years. They're the ones who tend to say they always wanted to:

- Lose 19 kg

- Find a life partner and have a family

- Emigrate and start a new life

- Write a book

- Start a successful business

- Run a marathon

- Be an Olympian

- You can fill in the gaps

It just never happened for them; they didn't get lucky.

It's not about luck. It's about the right kind of action. So many people procrastinate. They may claim that they are perfectionists, but all perfectionism is, is procrastination in disguise. It's a stalling tactic so they don't have to face up to the fact that their limiting belief might be right: they aren't good enough; are a failure; are not intelligent enough, worthy enough, loved enough. The list goes on.

When you create specific future memories, you clear the limiting beliefs. The handbrake is off and it's all systems go.

Dr Tad James, who invented Timeline Therapy™, which my team and I use for Seize Your Life, studied with the Huna tribe in Hawaii. They were revered historically as a tribe who could predict the future, but when Tad went to study with them, he realised they did not actually predict it; they created it.

Powerful stuff.

Not only do we need to communicate clearly with the unconscious mind what it is that we want, we need to make it specific. Imagine that I invited you to come to Portugal sometime in the next year. It would be lovely to spend time in the Algarve, but you'd get a sense that there's nothing about this invitation that you can really hang your hat on. You certainly wouldn't change anything in your near future to accommodate this trip because there is nothing solid or concrete about it; it's just a suggestion that may or may not happen.

When people are 'dreaming' about their future, this is what happens. It's too vague. Nothing is tangible or specific, so the plan will probably never happen.

If I were to say to you that on 21 May next year, you will be landing into Faro airport at 9am. A car will be ready to collect you and bring you to a villa next door to ours with its own private swimming pool. Once you've arrived and settled in, Sarah and I will then take you for lunch at one of our favourite beach restaurants where we can feast on the delights of the simple food of the Algarve.

Over the next four days, we will be taking a deep dive into some neural coding mind hacks and helping you to understand what you are capable of. The last three days will be free for you to do what you wish, maybe take a boat trip on the ocean or a road trip inland to visit some of the vineyards.

This is totally different. You will already have created some sense of a movie. Maybe you've imagined what the villa would feel like or what the lunch would taste like, imagined your flight or what Portugal smells like (orange blossom, by the way). You have been given specifics and these are what help you to create future memories in detail using an array of senses. The choices and actions you now take will be in alignment with this trip to Portugal. It is tangible. It's happening.

When you are designing your future, don't leave it to chance. Don't leave it to the tide to take you wherever it is going; avoid being the cork. Get specific about what it is that you want. Make sure it is positive, as in it's really what you want, not what you don't want. Make sure it increases your life and choices, that it will be good for everyone around you. You are then good to go with creating your own future memory.

What will you see, hear, feel (literally, not an emotional feeling), smell, taste? What will your internal dialogue be? Imagine this movie over a few times and notice how it makes you feel emotionally. Once the movie can run easily with all the elements – visual, audio, internal dialogue all generating emotional feelings, which should be powerful and strong – then you have created your future memory.

JOHN CONQUERS HIS EVEREST

Let's revisit John.

AMANDA: Tell me what you will be doing when you know you have done your swim the way you want to swim it?

JOHN: I will be standing at the bar in the surf club with my friends, just about to have a beer.

AMANDA: Great. What will you see?

JOHN: My friends around me, the bar, people celebrating and the beer, of course.

AMANDA: What can you hear?

JOHN: My friends saying, 'Well done, mate, you did it.'

AMANDA: What will you be saying to yourself?

JOHN: I've done it, I have conquered my Everest. I am so pleased.

AMANDA: What can you physically feel?

JOHN: The cold beer in my right hand.

AMANDA: Can you taste and smell anything?

JOHN: I can smell the beer, but I haven't tasted it yet.

AMANDA: Good. Now, close your eyes and let's start creating this movie. Run it from start to finish with all the elements in it and tell me when you have finished.

JOHN: OK.

John closes his eyes and runs his movie. His breathing is calm; he has a soft smile on his face and he takes his time.

He opens his eyes and tells me how great that felt. I can see this is a powerful future memory. Everything about him is calm and relaxed.

We run this movie three times, each time making it more and more powerful. I ask him to notice two things in his future memory he has not noticed before. He tells me the T-shirt he is wearing is the finisher's T-shirt, which is white, and there is condensation running down the beer glass. We then used Timeline Therapy™ the process developed by Dr Tad James, which allows us to use our unconscious mind to create future memories and remove negative emotions, to put this out into his future and that is the session over.

After his swim two days later, he sends me an email saying that he did it, he loved it and felt so calm and in control in the water. He also sends me a photograph taken by his friends. It was exactly as he had described in the future memory he created two days before his swim.

You have cleared your limiting belief and installed your new empowering belief, so now you are all systems go to design your future. Get designing, create your future, use your active imagination just as John did. Hop to the 'Further Resources' at the back of the book and I will take you through this personally via video. It will take around ten minutes, that's all.

That's not my movie!

You know that Sarah and I are married. You also know that I needed to fly to the United Kingdom to be with

Dad, who we sadly lost just after I landed. One thing I didn't share earlier is this part of the journey. This is better shared here at the end of the book, now you have all the tools.

When I was in the United Kingdom organising my dad's celebration of life, Sarah was still in New Zealand. Heavily pregnant, she had been given a fit-to-fly certificate and was going to fly to Europe alone, but her blood pressure started to escalate and her certificate was revoked. The babies were going to have to be born in New Zealand.

We had not planned this. She was due to give birth in Faro via C-section. All our baby things were in Portugal; in New Zealand, we had nothing.

After the celebration of life for my dad, I flew to New Zealand and the babies were delivered naturally (four minutes apart). Polly Weston and Anne Dymond, our obstetrician and midwife, were superb. We knew we were in good hands. The experience was beautiful, humorous, full of love, and yet the scariest thing we had ever done.

We were calling our family to share the news with them when the registrar checked on Sarah. She'd had a postpartum bleed, had lost around 3.5 litres of blood in thirty minutes and needed to go to surgery immediately.

Polly came rushing back in after a long night delivering the boys and I just had to wait. Losing Sarah was a real possibility. I sat there in the Newborn Intensive Care Unit, holding my two tiny sons and speaking out loud.

'This is not my movie. I do not drive home with these two boys alone. She has to make it.'

My future memory of us arriving home with the babies together, raising them together, being parents together was so strong that this could not be the new movie.

Sarah went into surgery at 7.15am and came into the Intensive Care Unit (ICU) at 12.30pm. It was a long wait, but she survived. That she made it was down to Polly's expertise. She had literally saved Sarah's life; it was touch and go.

The next forty hours were critical. Sarah stayed in the ICU for the next three days, while I brought the boys up to her so she could hold them, see them.

We are so grateful for every moment we have together with our boys. Life could have been very different. The tools that I have shared with you have helped us so much. Without them, I am not sure how we would have handled this curveball.

I can promise you that whatever comes your way, you will be much more resilient with the new knowledge and learnings that you now have.

You made it!

I want to thank you for staying with me; for learning how you can help you, take off the handbrake and climb into the world I am passionate about: belief change. You will now have much more awareness. You probably know your limiting and empowering beliefs, as well as having a clear idea of what your future memories are and how to put them out into your future. You will know when you are at cause or stuck in effect.

If you haven't done anything about your belief change yet, then breathe. That's OK, it is all about timing. You have dug deep and discovered more about you. Just this level of self-awareness will make a huge difference.

Please let me know what you thought of the book. My details are in the 'Author' section, so if there's anything you wish to have clarity on or just want to share, reach out. I am here. Alternatively, use #ichangedmybelief and I will find you.

Life is short. It is a gift, so go live it.

Gorge yourself.

Further Resources

Chapter 1

Dijksterhuis, Ap and Nordgren, Loran F, 'A theory of unconscious thought', *Perspectives on Psychological Science* (2006), 95–109, www.researchgate.net/publication/254124133_A_theory_of_unconscious_thougt, accessed August 2022

Hill, N, *Think And Grow Rich* (Vermillion, 2004)

Just Be Me course, https://yourlifeliveit.com/course/just-be-me-nlp-course

Martine Wright website, https://martinewright.co.uk

Chapter 2

Abbasi, K, 'A riot of divergent thinking', *Journal of the Royal Society of Medicine*, 104/10, (2011), 391, www.ncbi.nlm.nih.gov/pmc/articles/PMC3184540/, accessed August 2022

Carlsberg Cinema Prank (YouTube, 2011), www.youtube.com/watch?v=590pXIlr1Yc, accessed August 2022

Dyslexia Foundation of New Zealand, *Belief Change: The Family Journey* (DFNZ, no date), www.dfnz.org.nz/beliefchange.php, accessed August 2022

James, Tad, *Beyond Belief*, https://beyondbeliefthemovie.com/tag/tad-james/

Chapter 3

Krippendorff, K *Driving Innovation from Within: A guide for internal entrepreneurs* (Columbia Business School, 2019)

Chapter 4

Children Learning Reading.org, *The Story of a Mom Who Raised the Inventor of the Light Bulb* (Children Learning Reading.org, no date), www.childrenlearningreading.org/blog/thomas-edison-story.html, accessed August 2022

Feloni, R, 'Richard Branson explains the most important lesson he learned from his mom – and it included being pushed out of the car at age 6', *Business Insider* (16 November 2016), www.businessinsider.com/richard-branson-mom-taught-him-take-risks-2016-11, accessed August 2022

Chapter 5

Lipton, Bruce, *The Biology of Belief: Unleashing the power of consciousness, matter and miracles* (Hay House, 2010)

Chapter 7

Egan, B, *Winter Olympics: Margaux Hackett a stronger athlete after mental health struggles* (Stuff, 2022), www.stuff.co.nz/sport/olympics/300479137/winter-olympics-margaux-hackett-a-stronger-athlete-after-mental-health-struggles, accessed August 2022

Chapter 8

Brown, D, *Intervention: Finding patterns in randomness* (YouTube, 2014), www.youtube.com/watch?v=E8R8iWgjiIk, accessed August 2022

DiSalvo, David, 'Your brain sees even when you don't', *Forbes* (22 June 2014), "http://www.forbes.com/sites/daviddisalvo/2013/06/22/

your-brain-sees-even-when-you-dont/?sh=309d27af116a", access August 2022

Hypnosis audios, https://bit.ly/KnowingYouAudios

Walford, Olivia, *SleepTalk* (Hypnotherapist in Melbourne, 2019), https://hypnotherapistinmelbourne.com.au/service/sleeptalk/#:~:text=Created%20by%20Joane%20Goulding%20and,child%20development%20tools%20ever%20created, accessed August 2022

Chapter 9

Find your Neural Coder, https://yourlifeliveit.com/coaches

If you are a coach who wants to learn how to do belief change, please visit https://yourlifeliveit.com/course/online-the-ultimate-transformational-course

Chapter 10

Chopra, D, *Quantum Healing: Exploring the frontiers of mind/body medicine* (Bantam Dell, revised edition, 2015)

Pugh, L, *First Swim Across the North Pole* (YouTube, 2012), www.youtube.com/watch?v=WNmY_EAoXnU&t=19s, accessed August 2022

Put your future memory out into your timeline, https://vimeo.com/44772162/609ba7c5b3

Seize Your Life course, https://yourlifeliveit.com/course/seize-your-life-online-course

Acknowledgements

To my family, Noah, Jasper and Sarah, for your patience and understanding while I've been away in the early hours, writing this book in our VW camper-van. Thank you; I love you.

To my family and friends, who give us so much love, support and throw the logs of passion onto our bon-fire of life.

To all my clients who have taught me so much. Your growth inspires me. This book is richer because of your stories: real stories from real people who have given me permission to share their change and growth with my readers.

To my teachers, my gurus, my endless learning from all walks of life, thank you.

To all my students. You make my life richer, push me to deliver my best when teaching life-changing tools. Thank you.

And finally, to our Your Life Live It family. Together we are stronger, and I am grateful for each and every one of you.

The Author

Dr Amanda Foo-Ryland is a mother and wife, and the founder of Your Life Live It. She lives in Portugal and spends some time in New Zealand, which she loves. She is the author of two books, is a TEDx speaker and writes for various columns and publications. She is passionate about change work and letting people know that change can be both fast and long lasting.

Your Life Live It was founded in 2008 and has many Neural Coders who are part of the company, working with thousands of clients around the globe daily.

In her spare time, Amanda loves to run.

You can connect with Amanda:
amanda@yourlifeliveit.com

⊕ www.yourlifeliveit.com

For more about Amanda and group belief change work within business: https://creatingdreamteams.com/

🔲 https://m.facebook.com/yourlifeliveit/

🔲 http://linkedin.com/in/amandafoo-ryland

Amanda's Ted Talk: https://youtu.be/L4UTIsnY3-Q

Printed in Great Britain
by Amazon

If you think personal change is challenging, takes too much time, is expensive or can only come in pill form, think again.

Knowing You takes you on a shockingly simple journey of self-discovery. Packed with case studies and practical examples, this book shows that change can be achieved easily from within. It's not magic: it's neurology.

Find out how to:

- Stop blaming yourself and procrastinating, and understand how your brain works

- Identify, understand and delete limiting beliefs

- Become your own belief architect and design empowering beliefs that will serve you

- Achieve unthinkable change that transforms your life forever

Dr Amanda Foo-Ryland is a TedX and international keynote speaker and author. She founded Your Life Live It in 2008 and she and her team work with thousands of clients around the globe to help them to achieve unthinkable personal change that's fast and lasts. Learn more at www.yourlifeliveit.com

£13.99
US $18.99
€16.99

Panoma
a Rethink Press company

www.rethinkpress.com

PERSONAL
DEVELOPMENT

ISBN 978-1-78452-977-2

90000

9 781784 529772

THE FATE OF STARS

SEA AND STARS
BOOK ONE

SD SIMPER